"This is an epoch-making book. It is one of the most incisive memoirs ever written on the experience of mental illness, and by far the best first-person account available on life from the point of view of the OCD sufferer. Jeff Bell has scaled the heights of narrative memoirs, conveying the excruciating details of the inner life of a man whose brain is on fire."
—Jeffrey M. Schwartz, M.D., author of *Brain Lock* and *The Mind and the Brain*

"In a most sensitive way, Jeff Bell explains what it's like to be inside of his own self-made prison and describes his efforts to heal himself. His emphasis on his own spirituality and his willingness to change his attitude will shine light on the road to recovery for the many people afflicted with this disorder."
—Gerald G. Jampolsky, M.D., author of *Love Is Letting Go of Fear*

Rewind, Replay, Repeat

A Memoir of
Obsessive-Compulsive Disorder

Jeff Bell

HAZELDEN

Hazelden
Center City, Minnesota 55012-0176
1-800-328-0094
1-651-213-4590 (Fax)
www.hazelden.org

Library of Congress Cataloging-in-Publication Data
Bell, Jeff, 1963-
    Rewind, replay, repeat: a memoir of obsessive-compulsive disorder / Jeff Bell.
    p. cm.
    ISBN: 978-1-59285-371-7
    1. Bell, Jeff, 1963—Mental health. 2. Obsessive-compulsive disorder—Patients—Biography. I. Title.
    RC533.B45 2007
    362.196'852270092—dc22
    [B]

                                                    2006050118

Reprint permissions:
"This Is It," words and music by Kenny Loggins and Michael McDonald, copyright©1979 Milk Money Music and Tauripin Tunes. Lyrics reprinted on pages 137, 209, and 232 by permission of Alfred Publishing Co., Inc. All rights reserved.

Editor's note:
This book includes the author's personal accounts of living with obsessive-compulsive disorder. In some cases names, dates, and circumstances have been changed to protect anonymity. While every attempt has been made to provide accurate information in regard to OCD, this book is sold with the understanding that the publisher and author are not engaged in rendering psychological or other professional services. If expert counseling is needed, the services of a competent professional should be sought.

11 10 09   6 5 4 3 2

Cover design by Theresa Gedig
Typesetting and interior design by Prism Publishing Center

For
Samantha,
Nicole, and Brianna

In a world of doubts,
you are my certainty.

Belief consists in accepting
the affirmations of the soul . . .

Ralph Waldo Emerson

Foreword

As best I can figure, I have logged some eight thousand hours behind a studio microphone: not an unusual stat, really, for someone who has anchored radio news programs for well over a decade. What might be construed as a little odd—okay, downright weird—is this: unlike any other news anchor I know, *I* have recorded nearly every one of my on-air hours and have played back countless segments for myself. Why? To understand *that* is to understand the complexities of a cross-wired brain that would also have me check and recheck doors, appliances, facts and figures of all kinds, wobbly chairs and other serious hazards and, well, everything I have ever seen, heard, said, or done.

I myself don't even pretend to understand those brain complexities. I've read all about the myriad theories offered up by the world's top neuroscientists, who, despite their fascination with people like me, have yet to agree on an explanation for our many bizarre challenges. Faulty neurotransmitters? Frontal lobe abnormalities? Issues with our caudate nuclei? Beats me. I know nothing about neurology. Nothing about behavioral psychology. Very little, really, about the science behind obsessive-compulsive disorder (OCD), the diagnosis affixed to "checkers" like myself and an assortment of others battling hiccupping brains. *My* expertise is in doubt—which I suppose is the perfect double-claim for a pathological doubter. On the one hand, I can say with great confidence that I've lived a life more steeped in uncertainty than anyone I've ever run across, and along the way have compiled a virtual compendium of each and every one of its debilitating components. On the other hand, who am I not to doubt this very expertise? I mean, how can I be sure I really know anything about doubt? Or for that matter, about anything at all?

Reporters are taught to question everything, and perhaps this explains how and why I wound up in the news business. My biological predisposition to distrust and challenge has served me well in my professional life and has helped me get to the bottom of many a story. For this I am thankful, but not nearly so much as I am for the far greater gift my disorder has offered: endless lessons in the mechanics of believing. It's the ultimate paradox, yet somehow it also seems to add up—in much the same way, I imagine, that the deaf and the blind learn to hone their remaining senses.

I have all five of *my* senses, but tend not to trust any of them. Take touch and sight in their most basic functions. At my worst, I can be holding a parking brake in my hand, *seeing* it fully secure and *feeling* it locked and immovable; yet the moment I let go or look away, I lose all comprehension of its fixed condition. I can rattle, re-rattle, and re-re-rattle the handle, double back to my car a dozen times; and still there is no convincing myself, no means of storing my sensory input or warding off later doubt-driven urges to "replay" the whole sequence in my head, again and again. And so it is with far too many day-to-day challenges. Out of sheer necessity, I suppose, I have learned to believe beyond the limitations of my brain's flawed processing, to trust in the certainty of something much bigger than myself.

What follows is my story: one of some four to six million OCD stories unfolding right now in the United States. Like most, it's a tale of fear and torment and agony and shame. But *un*like far too many, it is also a story of triumphs, breakthroughs, miracles, and hope, and for this I can thank what I've come to call my "crash course in believing" and the remarkable "faculty" of professionals, friends, and unseen strangers who rescued me from the depths of my own looping hell.

Funny, but for a guy who's made a career of reporting on everything from floods and fires to heroes and crooks, I must confess that telling this story—*my* story—has challenged me like none other. In the end, I've decided there's only one way to share it, and that's by replaying on paper those well-worn segments of virtual audio and video I keep archived in my head, "tapes" much like my cassette recordings—"airchecks," as we in radio call them—of the eight thousand hours I've logged behind a studio microphone.

one

rewind to start

I am seven years old, maybe eight—it's hard to tell from the only fuzzy images I still have of this night. All I know for sure is that I'm an anxious young kid lying awake in bed, that my eyes are squeezed shut and my head is pounding, and that this is where the "tapes" begin.

It is sometime back in the early 1970s, this particular night, and I am passing its long hours deep beneath my covers, trying to make sense of the pictures I keep looping through my mind. There's a moving gray car, and a boy in the backseat leaning out the window, shouting something to me as I walk with my mother and sister down San Mateo Avenue. And then there's a shot of me stopping cold in my tracks, ratcheting my neck a full ninety degrees as the mysterious voice whizzes by. Over and over again, I am replaying these sequences, along with a looped track of the boy's "*Heeeeyyyyyy*" trailing off like a train whistle as the gray car disappears down the street.

I am doing all this because I have no other choice. Two days have come and gone since the scene with the passing car played out for real, and I have filled them with every possible effort to determine just who was trying to get my attention, and why. I have grilled my mother and sister, but neither even noticed the car or the voice on San Mateo Avenue. I have asked all my friends, hoping one of them might have been the boy in the backseat, but each has assured me he wasn't. So now I'm left with no viable option but to try to re-create for myself the ten or so seconds that hold all my answers.

The pictures come without effort for me, probably because of all the practice I've had. The Vietnam War is playing nightly on TV sets everywhere, and at bedtime for months now I've taken to conjuring up and playing back the haunting black-and-white war footage my parents watch over dinner. Soldiers marching through swamps. Bombs dropping, sending everything on our tiny screen flying. I hate the vivid images and the *what-if* questions they always

2

raise when I'm trying to fall asleep: *What if I have to go to war? What if I have to kill another human being? What if I die—what happens to me then?* Still, I'm certain that all kids must battle this problem, so I learn to work around the moving war pictures night after night.

The passing car images are different, though. They aren't violent like the Vietnam ones. They don't even scare me. But for some reason, they have even more power over me than the worst of the combat scenes. It's just something about how they taunt me, promising me the answers I'm looking for, if only I will take the time to review them carefully enough.

I can't see a reason not to, so I squeeze my eyes even tighter and I play back the whole scene yet again.

And again.

And again.

There are footsteps in the hallway now. Mom must be turning out lights and locking up our house for the night. This is my big chance.

"Mommy?"

The footsteps stop. I can tell my mother is standing in my doorway. "You're supposed to be sleeping," she whispers. "It's nearly eleven o'clock."

"I still can't figure it out," I mumble from beneath my covers.

"Figure what out?"

"The boy in the car."

Mom says nothing, so I pull back the blanket from my head and look up at her. "San Mateo Avenue? The kid who yelled something?"

"Sweetheart, we've already gone over all this," Mom says.

"I know."

My mother stares at me for a second or two, then tilts her head a bit to the side. "You've run out of things to worry about again, haven't you, sweetie?" It's the standing joke in our house: *Jeff gets worried when he has nothing to worry about.*

"You don't understand," I throw back at her.

She shakes her head. "No, honey, I guess I don't. Are you afraid that someone is going to hurt you?"

"No."

"That someone was out to scare you?"

"No."

"Then why can't you just accept that someone you know was trying to say hi?"

"Because I *neeeed* to know who that was."

"But *why?*"

She has me there. I don't have an answer. I don't know *why.* I look away in silence.

"Honey, I'm sure this isn't what you want to hear," she finally says, "but chances are you will never know."

No! Don't say that, I want to yell at my mother. *Tell me anything about the boy and the car. But*

4

please, I'm begging you, don't tell me that I'm never going to know.

"Okay," I mutter instead and kiss my mother goodnight.

I wait for the last light in the house to go out and the footsteps to stop. I pull the covers back up. Then I squeeze my eyes shut once more and, in my head, I back up the passing car yet again.

two

fast-forward 22 years

It's a shame, really, that I have to skip over such a big chunk of my life here. In so many ways, these were my best years, the ones I've come to think of as my "normal years." The kid who lay awake night after night replaying one image sequence after another somehow managed to morph into a pretty typical teen. For reasons I may never understand, the need for certainty that plagued me in my earliest memories just went away, poof, disappearing as mysteriously as it had hit me. Precisely when I can't remember, but by the time I'd reached high school I'd become your classic adolescent overachiever:

captain of the wrestling team, editor of the school paper, vice president of the student body, valedictorian of our senior class, yada yada.

Then came college. Southern California. Summer jobs teaching windsurfing lessons on Newport Bay. Samantha—my college sweetheart who would become my wife. And, in the end, a degree in engineering. Four wonderful years. Normal years.

Grad school next. An MBA. The unglamorous but exhilarating start of a career in radio. Two more normal years.

A wedding. Honeymoon in Greece. The birth of Nicole, our precious baby girl. A slow but steady climb up the ladder of commercial radio. Normal. Normal. Normal. Normal.

I cherish these years and would love nothing more than to write about them, but, alas, their only real contribution to this story is the precise hour to which they led me, an hour I've come to think of as the very last one of my normal years, and one that begins, appropriately enough, with my full attention focused on an aircheck.

K-S-F-O . . . San Francisco, Oakland, San Jose . . . News and information . . . It's ten o'clock . . . .Good morning, I'm Jeff Bell.

Yes. *Yes!*
I am pounding my steering wheel and talking

back to the familiar voice booming from the speakers of my Honda Civic. Just over two hours have passed since I wrote, produced, and anchored KSFO-AM's ten o'clock newscast. Now, thanks to the cassette tape playing back in my car stereo, I am hearing it for myself, savoring the sound of my own words, cocky with the knowledge that a nearby tower recently broadcast these very words to some six million potential listeners in the Greater San Francisco Metropolitan Radio Market.

I have put my entire life into this newscast. At least that's how it feels as I make my way down the Bayshore Freeway toward Oyster Point Marina this blustery fall afternoon, reliving my finest few minutes yet on KSFO and taking a mental inventory of my six years in radio. What a road it has been. Just months ago, I was going nowhere at a struggling coastal California station in market number two-hundred-and-something, living from paycheck to paycheck, dreaming of the big leagues, and sending airchecks and resumes to every program director I could find.

And now here I am.

San Francisco.

Market number four.

My hometown to boot.

. . . President-elect Bill Clinton is . . .

The voice on my aircheck is talking now about the '92 election. "A new beginning," Clinton is promising. I know this big break at KSFO is going to be mine. Sure, it's only nine hours of weekend airtime right now, but this is just the start. Weekends today, week*days* tomorrow. I'm certain that it's only a matter of time now before KSFO or some other top San Francisco station brings me on full-time. Then I'll be able to quit my overnight news writing job at Channel 2 TV during the week and focus all my attention on radio and getting—

. . . and that's the news. I'm Jeff Bell on
K-S-F-O five-sixty. . .

Whoa. Hang on. Too fast. I'm slurring the call letters. *Aren't I?* I stop the tape, back it up, hit Play again.

. . . on K-S-F-O five-sixty. . .

No, I'm okay. The pacing is good. I sound fine. Better than fine. Downright good. In fact, hearing my name that close to those legendary call letters— the same ones Jim Lange spelled out for years before moving to television as host of *The Dating Game*—I haven't a doubt in the world that I am officially off and running, well on my way to becoming one of the biggest radio news stars this city has ever seen.

And there ain't nothin' that can stop me now.

My new radio gig shouldn't mean so much to me, and I shouldn't be so damn cocksure about my future. I know better. But then again, I can't help it. At twenty-nine, I have everything I could ask for: the perfect marriage, perfect child, and now the perfect fast track to the top of the perfect profession.

And then there's the timing—everything coming together right here and right now in such a homecoming sort of way. Eleven years ago, my classmates at a high school just down the road voted *me,* a quirky, high-strung overachiever, "Most Likely to Succeed," a title forever sealed with a sappy picture in the yearbooks they no doubt either stashed away in closets or lost within weeks. Never even once did I give it another thought until moving back to the Bay Area last December. But now, I can't help thinking, I have finally earned my title.

If they could see me now.

Better yet, if they could *hear* me now.

And, oh yeah, thanks to KSFO's colossal signal, they can!

Before I even realize it, I am pounding the steering wheel again, an arrogant smile stretched across my face. It's still every bit there twenty minutes later as I pull into Oyster Point and see Samantha and Nicole waiting for me on The Boat.

PAUSE The Boat, capital T, capital B. It dawns on me that I should pause here a moment and share with you a few things you'll need to know about my father's sailboat for the rest of my story to make any sense.

For starters, there's the fact that, despite the proper name adorning its transom, Dad's thirty-foot sloop was referred to in our family simply as The Boat: a convenience, perhaps, but also a subtle, deferential nod to its central role in our lives.

For so many years, you see, The Boat could best be described as my father's shrine to perfection. From its meticulously stained woodwork to its ever-polished fiberglass hull, everything about The Boat—all thirty feet of it—was perfect. Of course, the same could be said about Dad's various cars over the years, or his airplane or motorcycle or any of the other possessions he held so dear. But The Boat had always stood above the rest as the ultimate in perfection, and even the slightest compromises to that perfection had triggered huge family ordeals. I spent at least a full decade hating The Boat and everything it represented.

You should also know, though, that by the early 1990s this was ancient family history. By then, The Boat was resting mostly unused in her slip, still well maintained but hardly perfect, and Dad himself seemed to be loosening his grip on perfection. We were both adults now, trying to redefine a father-son relationship that had been awkward at best for years. In so many ways, The Boat was the perfect vehicle, and I couldn't help seeing Dad's repeated invitations to use it as subtle messages that things were different now.

I'm sure neither one of us could have understood just *how* different things were about to become.

PLAY At 1:15, three friends of ours arrive at Oyster Point for what we billed as a quick tour of the Bay. Matt and Linda are a couple Samantha met through her paralegal work. Josh is a college buddy of mine who lives in the City. None of them has any sailing experience, but I assure them that's not an issue. I've been piloting boats, big and small, since I was barely tall enough to reach their tillers. An autumn day-sail like the one we've planned for today is routine.

Besides, I am meticulous, anal even, in my approach to boating, much as I am in my approach to everything I choose to take on. Sam calls this quality about me endearing; others, I'm guessing, find it obnoxious. Whatever the case, it's why I've gone to great lengths to prep and supply the boat for this trip, like so many in the past, and why I've taken the time to think everything through. Everything, that is, except for what happens next.

A sputter.

That's how it all starts, really—with a smoke-belching sputter, a mechanical cough of sorts, just seconds after I back The Boat and our crew out of the slip. I am sliding the two-way gear shift from reverse to forward, ready to swing the bow around as I've done a hundred times before. But something's not right. All too soon that something becomes all too apparent. The engine is dead.

Shit. This has never happened before. I fumble with the controls and within a minute have the engine restarted. But it's too late. The wind has already delivered us to the row of boats just across the narrow waterway.

"Get on the starboard side and fend off," I holler like a madman to my crew of landlubbers, none of whom even knows the starboard side of a boat from its port.

Kenny, the guy in the slip next to ours, does his best to be helpful. "Throw the rudder all the way over," he shouts.

Another guy appears out of nowhere on the deck of the cabin cruiser we are about to hit. He, too, is yelling suggestions. The sudden confusion in my head drowns them both out. I lose my bearings and, in a moment of panic, add throttle when I should be backing it off.

Grrrrrrr. Our starboard aft scrapes the end of a dock, which creaks its defiance. Our starboard bow closes in on the cabin cruiser. For what must be seconds but feels like hours, a tangle of arms and legs fights to keep the two boats apart. Finally, we are clear of trouble. I shout a "Thank you" and "Sorry!" to the guy on the cabin cruiser, and we are on our way.

No harm, no foul—or so I'm convinced.

Embarrassed and shaking, I apologize to our guests. "Thank God we didn't make any contact," I mutter just loud enough for my own two ears, never intending for a second to throw the issue open for debate.

"I dunno," Matt volunteers. "I think we may have bent the nose of that boat."

With instinctive panic, I swing around to face Matt. "Which boat, the cabin cruiser?" I hear myself sounding defensive, but it's only because I was right there in the cockpit the entire time, watching every second of our mishap unfold, and *I* sure hadn't seen any hull-to-hull contact. *"Bent the nose"—what does he mean by that?* The growing knot in my gut reaches grapefruit size as I press Matt for details.

"Do you think we've done any permanent damage?"

"No, nothing like that," he reassures me, explaining that he'd heard some creaking and just assumed we "temporarily bent that wood thing that sticks out from the bow."

He is talking about a bowsprit, a pronounced

feature I don't remember that cabin cruiser having. As for the creaking, I'm convinced that had to have come from the dock; I heard it myself.

For three hours on the Bay, I go through the motions of playing captain to our guests, doing my best to be a gracious host and pointing out the highlights of our tour. When the conversation turns to Bay Area media, as it always seems to these days, I try to act the part of rising radio star. But I am distracted, lost deep inside myself, preoccupied with a voice in my head. It is Matt's, repeating itself relentlessly: *I think we may have bent the nose of that boat. I think we may have bent the nose of that boat. I think we may have bent the nose of that boat . . .*

Back at the dock, Matt and Linda thank us for an enjoyable afternoon and then head for the parking lot along with Sam and Nicole. I waste no time grilling Josh, one-on-one, for his thoughts. He'd been right there next to Matt during all the confusion and *he* hadn't seen or heard any signs of damage.

"If we made any contact at all," he tells me, "it had to have been minimal."

"Are you certain?"

"I'm certain."

"But do you think—"

Josh holds up a hand as if to stop traffic.

"Relax," he says. "Nothing happened. Honestly."

The two of us walk over to the cabin cruiser and do our best to assess things. A large blue canvas deck-cover conceals the boat's bow, but it isn't hard to figure out that it has no bowsprit to bend. *Matt had it all wrong*. Without pulling back the cover, we look around for any obvious signs of damage. This is no easy task given the dilapidated state of the boat; it is a harbor derelict by any definition. Still, the bow appears to be in good shape, and Josh convinces me everything is fine.

As we're about to leave, I notice a light on inside the cabin and knock to see if anyone is onboard. A disheveled guy about my age pokes his head out. I thank him for helping us at the dock this morning. He looks confused and says nothing, so I explain how our engine had died and how someone from his boat had helped fend us off.

"Must have been my partner," he decides. "I'll pass along your appreciation."

I should tell him about the creaking Matt heard, spell out my concern that we may have damaged his bow. But this guy, with his eyebrows cocked high, is giving us a dismissive look that all but shouts, *I don't have time for this—I've got a woman, or dinner, or something important down here that I need to get back to, and quickly.*

Now I am panicking. *Should I pass along Matt's theory, just in case?* I decide to buy a second or two with some lame compliment regarding his boat, but given its current state of disrepair, I find myself cringing at my own words just as soon as they come out.

"This old piece of crap?" he throws back at me before I can even finish.

"Well, looks like you're in the process of restoring it," I try.

"Yeah, maybe one of these days. Hey, I'll see you guys around."

And then he is gone.

Josh laughs under his breath and whispers to me, "I guess he had something *important* to do."

The two of us walk back to The Boat and polish out the small section of hull that had picked up some rubber residue from the dock. The sky is nearly dark as we say our good-byes.

■

I think we may have bent the nose of that boat. I think we may have bent the nose of that boat. I think we may have bent the nose of that boat. Nose of that boat. I think we may have . . . That boat. I think we may have bent . . .

It's the middle of the night, and Matt's voice is every bit as clear as it was live and in person hours ago. Like a looped audiotape, his words play over and over again in my head. The strangest part is that they aren't doing so of their own accord; somehow I am hitting the Play button. Over and over and over again. And I can't stop myself.

Ever since this afternoon I've been trying to shake the all-encompassing thought that I damaged the cabin cruiser and the even more disturbing notion that I'll never know for sure exactly what happened. Clearly, Matt had heard something, but what? The uncertainty of all this is unbearable, especially in the silence of my pitch black bedroom. I need answers. I need to know what Matt was thinking. My only clues are the very words that he himself had chosen to use, so I keep playing them back in an inane effort to better understand them.

The exercise gets me nowhere, and before long I find myself switching mediums, from virtual audio to virtual video. Now, instead of listening to Matt's words, I am watching the actual scene replay itself on the fuzzy screen inside my head. I can see myself fumbling with the controls. I can see the boat being blown across the way. Here's when the starboard aft makes contact with the dock, and there's the guy from the cabin cruiser. The critical scene is next, but damn it all, the shot is out of focus. For hours I replay the incident, looking for answers, but to no avail.

It must be two a.m. now and poor Sam looks even groggier than she did the last time I shook her awake fifteen minutes ago. I should let her go back to sleep, stop peppering her with questions about what she recalls from this afternoon. But I can't. I need to know what happened with the boats. Frustrated, Sam again asks me why I need to know. Again I try but fail to explain, and meanwhile a déjà-vu sensation starts tugging at my consciousness. It was long ago. There was a mysterious voice. My mother and I were having this awkward conversation, the first of many like it that we'd have during my childhood.

The moment passes and I again focus on the present. I try to shift gears, think instead about my big future in radio. But I know whatever it is I'm feeling right now about that, it's anything but cocky.

three

fast-forward 9 days

It's a little after seven and just a minute into the Wednesday edition of KTVU-TV's *Mornings on Two* program when I first realize something isn't right.

Fifty feet from my desk in the sprawling Channel 2 newsroom, Frank Somerville and Laura Zimmerman are giving voice to the words that I, as their news writer, have fed them via the teleprompter scripts rolling just in front of their set. Serious and concerned, our two anchors are peering into Camera One, updating a much-talked-about shooting on a local commuter train—our lead story this morning, and one our executive producer, Rosemarie, has entrusted me to write.

The problem is, at this same moment, a chorus of groans is rising across the newsroom. I have, it would seem, screwed up the story.

Like a desperate lawyer in a courtroom, I shuffle through my notes, scrambling to piece together my blunder. As best I can figure, the groans had started when Laura—or was it Frank?—mentioned that the victim had *died* from his gunshot wounds. Hadn't he?

Son of a bitch. It says right here in the wires that he's in critical condition.

And now, I know, so am I.

Screw-ups are inevitable in live TV. This, however, is a big one, and I'm all but certain I'll be hearing about—

"JEFF BELL. See me in the control room. *Jeff!*"

Rosemarie's voice punches through the newsroom loudspeakers like a right hook to the face. My face. The crowd goes wild without a sound, the way coworkers do when they get to witness a good knockout blow from the boss. If there was any doubt before as to just what idiot was responsible for the morning's egregious writing error, there isn't any longer.

"This *cannot* happen," Ro says, very matter-of-fact-like, as I pull up a chair next to her in the NASA-style control room that serves as command central for Channel 2's newscasts. I know this is going to be awkward; the two of us have always had a great working relationship.

"I am so sorry—" I start to say.

Ro looks up from her computer screen briefly, just long enough for me to see the disappointment written all over her face.

"This is just so unlike you," she says. "I guess I don't understand how you could let it happen."

I shake my head in mock bewilderment. I know damn well just how I've let it happen.

Two days later, Ro again summons me to the control room, again because I've managed to screw up another key story—this time giving a crucial newsmaker the wrong last name—and again I know exactly how I've managed to do it.

The problem is there's no way I can share this explanation with my boss.

What am I going to say? "Well, uh, here's the thing, Ro, as silly as this may sound, I, uh, I'm having some trouble concentrating because, well, because of these boats taking up all the space in my head." No way would she or anyone else ever understand if I explained that, instead of playing back the raw news footage I'm supposed to be reviewing, I am playing back my own personal tapes, and without the aid of our state-of-the-art video machines.

I've been doing this playback thing, mentally

re-creating the whole boat incident, almost nonstop since the mishap eleven days ago now. I do it in bed when I should be sleeping. I do it in the shower and while I'm shaving. And, although Ro is never going to hear this from me, I do it for eight hours a night at my computer terminal in the Channel 2 newsroom.

Play. Rewind. Play. Rewind.

The scariest part, and the thing I just don't get, is that I simply cannot stop myself—not even after seeing how destructive the whole attention-sapping process is. Somehow, the doubt keeps driving me back for more, like an evil whispering voice reminding me that if I can't figure it out now, I'll have to spend the rest of my life wondering what happened. *Are you really prepared to live like that, questioning forever whether the cabin cruiser might sink?*

"And here's the rest of it," I'd have to tell Ro. "I'm just not getting any sleep. None." The image playbacks, of course, have a lot to do with this. But there's another factor, too. Instead of going home for naps after my overnight shifts, I am spending my mornings back at the marina, looking for any physical clues that my virtual tapes can't provide.

For hours on end, I sit in my car in the marina parking lot, scoping out The Boat and the cabin cruiser, assessing their relative heights, the distance between them, and any and all other relevant measures. I take countless walks up and down the docks, trying to grasp just what had happened that fateful afternoon. I scour The Boat from its transom to its bow and back to its transom again, hunting for tangible signs of damage, for proof that Matt had been either right or wrong about our encounter. But most of all, I hide out below deck, just out of view of the rest of the harbor, staring off at the cabin cruiser berthed fifty feet across the waterway.

None of this feels right to me, especially when I find myself peering through binoculars at the cabin cruiser's bow, combing it inch by inch—while pretending to check weather conditions on the horizon, just in case I am caught. This is not normal behavior. I realize this. But much as I can't stop myself from replaying the looped images, I also can't seem to keep myself from taking one more walk along the dock or stealing one more peek at the bow through my high-powered field glasses.

On my way home from Channel 2 each morning, I try to keep going straight when I approach the Oyster Point exit on southbound 101, try to keep the steering wheel from turning slightly to the right. But I can't. I am no longer steering my own car or, for that matter, my own life. Fear and doubt are driving me now. Back to the scene of the crime again and again.

With each successive visit, the marina becomes more of a prison. It's almost as if I am doing time there, serving some kind of self-imposed sentence I don't understand. I want to stay away from the harbor when I'm not there, and *get away* from it when I am, but somehow neither is an option. And so I keep going back, always for what I promise myself will be a quick visit, and always for what turns out to be the better part of the day.

Sometimes, when I'm hiding out below deck and staring off into space, my worst childhood boat memories seem to flood the cabin, sweeping me back in time. I can see myself, a ten-year-old kid, scrambling to help Dad anchor The Boat behind a small island in the Sacramento Delta. Mom and I are in an inflatable life raft, rowing like crazy to drop the anchor where Dad wants it to be. But we haven't done it right, and Dad is shouting directions to do it again.

"Come on, goddammit, we haven't got all day!"

The Boat is swinging like a kite in the wind, so the pressure is on me, along with Mom—who is now covered with river mud and bruised from the anchor—to figure things out quickly. We give it our best shot, then row as fast as we can back to The Boat, where we help Dad and my sister, Mandi, pull the slack out of the anchor line hand over hand. Finally we are set.

And then again, perhaps we are not.

"Goddammit, son of a bitch, motherfucking . . ." My father is barking out a string of obscenities, as he does when things aren't going just as planned. The words are directed at no one in particular. Not Mom. Not Mandi. Not me. Just the world. Still, they are so charged, so full of venom, that each of us will do anything to fix whatever is wrong, to somehow find a way to make the words stop.

In this case, the anchor-line angles happen to be wrong. The buoy-bottle line still has too much slack in it.

Mom and I know what to do. We climb back into the life raft, row back to the buoy, hoist the heavy galvanized anchor back out of the water, and drop it back down to the river bottom once more.

Thankfully, the third time's the charm. But Mom and I have made a mess of the cockpit with all the thick mud from our legs and our feet. We'll need to scrub the decks just as soon as possible. I'm guessing we'll also need to polish the hull where the rubber raft is now banging into it. None of this is too serious, but what I discover next is: there, right in front of me, is a one-inch scratch in the fiberglass cockpit where the excess anchor chain now lies. Dad sees what I'm looking at and shakes his head. I hang mine low, knowing it was probably my fault. I have screwed up again, and again let down my father.

Maybe Dad should explain to Ro why I can't seem to get her news stories right.

■

Fall turns to winter before I know it, and Christmas, New Year's, and Valentine's Day roll through like San Francisco's fast-moving fog banks. I settle into a pattern, rationing my time-consuming playbacks at Channel 2, relishing my weekend airtime on KSFO, and doing my best to stay clear of The Boat.

Meanwhile I struggle to understand what has happened to me. How could I have spent three solid months consumed by a mistake I know is behind me? Yet the more time passes, the more guilty I feel. And the more guilty I feel, the more determined I grow to know what, if any, damage I've caused. I want more than anything to confess my concerns to the owners of the cabin cruiser. I have absolutely no evidence, though. No case to make to them.

■

In mid-March our extended family gathers at our house in San Bruno to celebrate Nicole's second birthday. She is on cloud nine with the attention. Samantha and I are glowing with pride. It's lunchtime, and a dozen or so of us are sitting around the table wearing ridiculous party hats, catching up on one another's lives. Soon the conversation turns to Dad's single-engine plane and the fact that someone at the airport recently put a ding in it without the common courtesy of leaving a note, making the whole thing, as he puts it, a true "hit and run."

BAM!

An invisible two-by-four smacks me over the head.

Oh my God, that's it, I decide. "Hit and run"—that's what *I* have done.

I am dizzy in an instant, and the voices around me become one loud buzz, as if I'm listening to them through a long cardboard tube. The room disappears as Nicole makes a face about something and all the adults start to giggle.

The conversation moves along to some other subject.

But I am frozen. My skin is clammy. I wonder for a second if I will actually pass out.

Fear. Shame. Guilt. Horror. A flood of emotions washes over me at once, but until I notice the salty taste at the corners of my mouth, I don't even realize that my eyes have started to leak. Fortunately, no one else at the table has noticed, so I excuse myself and make my way to the downstairs bathroom.

The tile floor is cold. But it's the only makeshift bed I have at my disposal. Curled up in a little ball now, I let it all out, trying only to muffle the sounds that might give me away.

So there it is: you may be guilty of a hit and run.

It's that familiar voice I've dubbed Doubt, the one that tells me I need to review my tapes, or pay another visit to The Boat in search of damage.

You've got to confess, it taunts. *Come clean now or you'll never sleep another night of your life.*

You're wrong, Doubt, I rationalize. The cabin cruiser owner was onboard at the time of the mishap. He even helped fend us off. Surely he would have been in the best position to know whether or not there was any serious contact.

Well, what if that man was just a passerby who climbed aboard the cabin cruiser to lend a hand and really didn't care what happened to the boat? The real owners may have no clue . . .

But Josh and I talked to someone aboard the cabin cruiser later that day, explaining exactly what had happened with our two boats.

You didn't mention the creaking . . .

But the two of us looked over the cabin cruiser together, and I've combed it with my binoculars countless times since. Never have I seen a single sign of any obvious damage.

Like you'd be able to spot the damage on an old wreck like that . . . and what if you're missing something?

Suddenly there's a tap on the door.

"Honey, are you all right?"

"Uh, yeah," I answer my clearly concerned wife. I check my watch and scramble to peel myself off the bathroom floor.

"We're ready to do birthday cake now. We're just waiting for you."

"Right. I'll, uh, be out in a second," I say, not knowing how I could possibly step out of this room even if I had the rest of the day to get ready.

four

fast-forward 1 month

"*Daaa*dy, I am *ask*ing you a question. Can-we-go-home-now?"

Nicole's voice is serious, concerned, a little frightened even.

"In a minute, sweetheart," I say, realizing I've stalled my answer as long as possible.

"I don't think Mommy would like this," she tells me again from her perch on top of my shoulders.

"But we're having fun, aren't we?"

Nicole says nothing. Her smile and giggles of a half hour ago are long gone now, and quite clearly, she *isn't* having fun anymore. Maybe it's the steady rain, which has drenched her clothes and long hair by this point. Perhaps it's just that we've been standing here on this dock for what must seem like forever.

I know this is stupid—keeping my shivering daughter outside in a downpour—but I'm on a mission, and she is my decoy. Of course, Nicole doesn't understand any of this; as far as she knows, we're just out admiring Grandpa's boat from across the way. This is special "Daddy and Nikki time," and it had sure started as a lot of fun. How could she know that I've carefully picked this observation point, the perfect place to stand with my cute little daughter, seemingly taking in the view of the boat one row over? Why would she ever guess that in reality Daddy is scouring the cabin cruiser next to us, searching again for any signs of damage?

It's the perfect undercover operation, really, brilliantly conceived and almost flawlessly executed. We are fooling everyone—not that there's a single person around in the entire soggy harbor to fool, certainly not one who would give a damn one way or the other. Still, I can't take any chances. People wouldn't understand. They'd think I'm crazy.

Nikki will just have to wait a little longer.

This is April, and I am squandering almost every day of it at Oyster Point Marina, slithering around like the conniving criminal I've come to consider myself to be. I still spend entire mornings combing The Boat from end to end and staring out at the cabin cruiser until my eyes go blurry. Frustrated by my lack of answers, I have also begun devising new and elaborate schemes for scoping out both boats, covert operations like the one on which I dragged Nicole. The irony, I am learning, is that the more I catch myself sneaking around, the guiltier I feel, and the more convinced I become that I've done something truly unforgivable.

II PAUSE Okay, chances are pretty good that, as a reader, you're beginning to cringe with each reference to The Boat about now. I know this from the feedback of well-meaning friends who read an early draft of this memoir and warned me that I risked losing the interest of "normal" people if I dwelled too long on my growing consumption with the boat mishap. "It's very tiring," they cautioned.

Tiring?! Hell-oh! I wanted to snap back at them. *You have no idea.* But here's the thing: somehow, some way, I need to give you—all of you—an idea of *tiring,* a taste of the grinding agony of having one's entire world reduced to a single all-encompassing fixation. Believe me, you're getting off easy. You've now spent some ten or fifteen minutes reading about The Boat episode. I, at this juncture, have thought about nothing else for more than 150 days. Every minute. Every day.

We'll move on. I promise we will. But—and I'm very sorry for this—we can't just yet . . .

▶ PLAY May 4, 1993. Almost six months to the day after The Boat's engine—and a big part of me—died in a sputter. It's a Tuesday morning, and I'm wrapping up my compulsory daily visit to Oyster Point Marina when a flash of reflected sunshine draws my attention to one of The Boat's many chrome stanchions.

And then I see it. Right in front of me. A small gouge, or at least a good-sized scratch, in the polished chrome roughly a foot and a half above the deck.

No!

I never thought to scour the stanchions for any signs of damage; my focus has always been the actual hulls of The Boat and the cabin cruiser.

Without even thinking, I squeeze my eyes shut and allow my tape of the whole boat mishap to play back for the millionth time. No stanchion anywhere. It's not in my line of sight from my place in the cockpit. But there is Matt, standing just inches from where the stanchion must be.

Suddenly it all makes sense. Our *stanchion* had made contact with the bow of the cabin cruiser that day. I even know precisely where, since the wind had recently blown back a corner of the blue canvas cover from the cabin cruiser's bow section, revealing what's known as an anchor plate, a solid chrome shield designed to accommodate heavy-duty anchor chain.

The creaking—it wasn't some nonexistent bowsprit, or any other piece of wood, bending under impact. It was our stanchion scraping across the anchor plate.

For a split second I'm relieved, having found at long last a plausible explanation. But then the reality sinks in: we *had* made contact. Matt *had* been right. My own eyes and ears had failed me.

If only I had checked more thoroughly!

Now, as if to make up for the six months of missing it, I simply cannot take my eyes off the scratch in front of me.

Ten minutes pass. And then another ten. And then at least ten more after that.

It's getting late and I need to get home. But I have a new problem now: I have to come clean, have to let the cabin cruiser owners know that I've found "damage." Never mind that The Boat's one-inch stanchion would've easily buckled or broken clean off before doing any harm to that massive anchor plate; we *had* made contact, and that is that.

■

At a little after ten the following morning, I pull into the Oyster Point parking lot and jump out of my car like a junkie in hot pursuit of his fix. My overnight shift at Channel 2 had been hell as I counted the hours until I could get myself back to the harbor. Now, making my way down the dock, I notice that someone is aboard the cabin cruiser, a young guy I've seen a few times before, but not the same one Josh and I had talked to that first day. Thank God *someone* is there, I think to myself. At least now I can get this confession over with as quickly as possible.

For two hours I tuck away in The Boat's cabin, waiting for the guy on board to leave for a bathroom visit or any other reason. This way I can casually bump into him on the dock and casually mention that I discovered a scratch. Just a casual conversation between a couple of fellow boaters. All very casual.

What I can't figure out though is the *pretense* for sharing this information with him, six months after an incident that someone else on his boat had showed zero interest in discussing. And if my stanchion-versus-anchor-plate theory is correct, how can I possibly suggest that we might have damaged his—

A moving figure on the horizon snaps me back to the moment. It's the guy on the cabin cruiser, looking as if he's about to head for the dock.

Decision time.

I don't want to do this, confront him now, and

make an ass of myself. But this inner voice, Doubt, tells me that I have no choice, that I couldn't possibly live with the uncertainty of never knowing whether someone with the cabin cruiser would want my information about our scratch. It also suggests that I'm the scum of the earth if I don't do the only right thing and confess my sins.

There *is* another inner voice trying to whisper to me, some rational part of myself that understands this is all just garbage. It tries to tell me that my motives have nothing to do with helping others or doing the right thing, that in truth I'm only hoping this confession will somehow silence my voice of doubt and allow me to stop playing back all my endless virtual tapes.

But this whisper of reason is all but inaudible.

I know I simply cannot stop myself. Not now. Not tomorrow. Not anytime soon. So instead I make a deal with my rational self: I will indulge my craving to come clean right here and right now. But I will also make some calls in the next few days— calls to arrange for professional help for my growing problems.

I step off the boat.

Our paths, mine and Cabin Cruiser Guy's, meet at the bottom of the main ramp leading up to the parking lot. I try my best to look casual, as if this encounter is purely by chance.

"Hey, how's it going?" I say with a quick nod of my head.

"Hey."

"My name's Jeff. I'm with the sailboat over there."

"Hey."

He is obviously a man of very few words. I, on the other hand, am one with a long string of them I can't wait to unleash.

"Listen," I say, "about six months ago I was backing our boat out of its slip when the engine died and the wind blew us over to your boat which we checked out just as soon as we got back and talked to someone on board and everything seemed to be fine but I thought you should know that I just found a scratch on one of our stanchions and now I'm concerned that maybe we did in fact do some damage to your boat and—"

Cabin Cruiser Guy is staring at me. Staring as one might examine with fascination a rare bird at the zoo. He doesn't know what to make of me, how to process what I am trying to tell him.

"I'm sure our boat is fine," he finally says.

Now *I'm* at a loss. This is not the indignant demand for reparations I'd been expecting, even hoping for, from him.

"Well, please let me know if you find any damage."

"Rrrright," he says, taking way too long to get the single syllable out of his mouth. It dawns on me that it's possible I'm actually scaring this guy.

The conversation is now complete. We both walk on along our own paths. Looking down, I see that my entire body is shaking.

Casual. Very casual.

Well, at least it's over with, I try to rationalize. Now I can get on with the rest of my life.

My sense of relief is tempered moments later, though, when I remember the bargain I'd just made with myself.

five

fast-forward 6 days

I suppose it's only fitting that the opening frames of my next tape segment would have me on El Camino Real, the historic six-lane thoroughfare spanning the San Francisco peninsula, and the very road I'll forever associate with permanent records.

Two decades earlier, while riding down El Camino in the back of my parents' Ford LTD station wagon, I'd watched my father get a traffic ticket and, within minutes, slip into a funk so deep and dark that it gave me shivers. I understood even back then what it was all about. Dad, after all, worked in the insurance business. He was always preaching to us about permanent records: how crucial they are to one's future, how many people and agencies have access to them, and most of all, how important it is to protect them at almost any cost. I knew that this ticket meant Dad's record was no longer perfect, and if I'd had any doubts before about the significance of a blemish, I never would again after seeing his reaction.

So now here I am, all grown up in 1993, heading down El Camino to an appointment certain to forever taint my own permanent record.

It's a Tuesday morning, and I am keeping my promise to myself, making good on the deal that allowed me to confess my sins to the guy from the cabin cruiser. It seemed like a fair trade-off at the time, but now, on my way to actually sit down with a "professional," I am realizing what a poor decision this was. I know Dad would think so—even if I succeed in keeping any trace of this visit off my permanent record.

My appointment is with Dr. X, a man I know nothing about except that he comes recommended by my only link to the counseling world: my mother. Mom is a high school guidance counselor, so she had seemed like a logical starting point when I'd set out to find a psychologist. It wasn't until I'd left her house that day that I realized the irony of a grown man turning to his own mother for advice in selecting a shrink. Now I can't help wondering if my decision might have had something to do with the very confession problem with which I need help.

I also wonder if Mom has shared our conversation with Dad.

Samantha says I shouldn't worry about any of this. That what I really need to do now is focus on getting myself better.

She never has understood the delicate dynamics that hold my family together.

■

Arriving early, it turns out, was not my best idea. While I'm fairly certain no one saw me park my car three blocks away, or snake my way on foot to this old brick building, I never anticipated I'd have company in the oversized closet that serves as a waiting area for the ground floor's several psychologists. Fortunately, the middle-aged woman sitting across from me and fidgeting like a kid at church seems every bit as intent as I am on remaining anonymous.

Following her cue, I bury my nose in an issue of *Newsweek*.

I am waiting for someone to call out my name. But it's five past eleven, and the door marked *Dr. X* hasn't cracked an inch. Is the last patient still in there? Am I supposed to get up and knock on the door?

Two more minutes pass. And then another. I am getting uncomfortable.

"Jeff?"

A stocky man in his fifties appears in the doorway. Did he really have to use my name like that, right here, out in public?

"Dr. X?" I ask. I am watching the fidgeter out of the corner of my eye.

"Yes. Come on in."

At least we're now moving this conversation behind closed doors.

"Make yourself comfortable," he says, as I step into the room.

But I can't find the couch. There isn't one anywhere. The doctor sees my confusion and points to a chair.

"You were expecting a sofa?"

"Well, it's just that I've never—"

"They only use those in movies," Dr. X says with a slight chuckle. I can tell he's trying to put me at ease. But I'm in no mood for chitchat or wisecracking comments.

"I need to ask you something, Doctor, before we get started."

"Shoot."

"Is anyone ever going to know about these conversations?"

"Not unless you tell me you're about to commit a crime."

Is that what he thinks? Why would he say that?

"No. No! It's just that I'm very concerned about word of our meetings ever getting out."

The doctor moves his pen now without looking down. I wonder if he's making some note on the legal pad on his lap.

"Counseling is a very confidential process," he tells me. "I truly don't think you have anything to worry about."

Yeah. Easy for him to say. No one's going to yank his career out from under him when they find out we've been talking.

"So how 'bout we start with what brings you my way."

This is my cue. Now I'm supposed to spill everything. I'll be damned though if I'm going to let my deepest, darkest secrets wind up on that yellow legal pad. Not a chance.

Confessing to my boat mishandling, on the other hand, is something I'm more than willing—perhaps even eager—to do. So that's where I start. I tell him the whole story, from the engine dying to my recent conversation with the cabin cruiser guy.

"So you've told these other boat owners about your concerns, twice now?" he asks when I'm done.

"Right. But I'm not convinced they understand that I might have damaged their boat."

"Sounds like they couldn't care less. From what

you've described, this old 'cabin cruiser' is a real piece of shit."

The doctor's choice of words might have caught me off guard, but I've already decided that everything about him seems to scream *tough guy*. His gestures. His expressions. Even the way he cocks his head.

I like this, for some reason. Yet I can't help wondering if he thinks I'm a sissy. Real men don't go whining to shrinks.

At 11:50, I figure out what Dr. X has been glancing at just above my right shoulder. It's a clock, telling him it's time to wrap up our conversation, which by this point has moved on to a quick overview of my life and my fast-track radio career.

I ask him what's next.

"Well, are you up for doing this again?"

I've already decided that he gets exactly four sessions to fix me. I tell him that, in so many words.

"Fine then," he says. "I'll see you next Tuesday."

◼

My second meeting with Dr. X begins much like the previous one, with a sweeping invitation.

"So what do you feel like talking about today?"

It's a loaded question, and I find myself thinking less about my answer than the expression on his face. Sincere, but macho. Very tough. Hey, big man, it seems to say, we're just a couple of guys shooting the shit. You can tell me anything. Go on now.

I'm not going to fall into his trap.

"I dunno."

"Well, this boat concern of yours. Let's start there. Tell me how it's affecting your life."

Uh-oh. *That's* where he's trying to take me now. No way. I'm not going to talk about all the crazy stuff I've been doing around the boat. And I certainly don't need him writing down something about "tapes" playing and replaying in my head. That's not the stuff for legal pads.

"It's very . . . *distracting*." I choose my words with great care.

"How so?"

"Well, the more time I spend worrying about the whole thing, the less time I have to devote to my radio career."

"Ah. Your career! You're having trouble accepting your success, aren't you?"

Huh? Where did *that* one come from? I tilt my head slightly and lift one eyebrow.

"It's a very common thing. You're young. Very successful. Everything's going your way."

"Yeah?"

"A lot of guys can't handle that. They need to find problems to distract themselves. I see it with young doctors, lawyers, all kinds of professionals your age."

Dr. X is on a roll now. He's figured everything out and is imparting his wisdom to me. *Fear of success,* he calls my problem. Says it's been around forever. Apparently, ancient tribes even had a ritual for dealing with it.

"I bet you were always a big overachiever," he says.

"No argument there." I'll play along. Beats talking about the stuff I should really be sharing.

We spend the rest of my fifty minutes discussing my high school and college honors, my athletic achievements, and my recent broadcasting success.

Lots of fuel for the good doctor's fire.

■

A few days later, Samantha and I learn of another success, one that has *her* beaming and *me* more concerned than ever about the future. According to the plus-sign on the plastic device she is holding, we are now eight months away from our second child.

I fake my delight as best as I can and, together with Sam, make calls to our closest family and friends. I am uneasy though, and my mind keeps flashing back three years, to the day Sam and I first learned we'd be parents. It was, as I recall so vividly now, both the most exciting and the most horrifying day of my life.

The excitement had come first, in the form of ecstasy and wonder. I remember holding Samantha tight, the two of us contemplating our lives ahead as real-life parents.

But what I remember most is the bizarre question that popped into my head just a few minutes later: *What if I already have kids out there, bastard children I don't know that I've fathered? What if one of my old girlfriends got pregnant but never told me?*

It was the strangest, most illogical notion, especially considering that I had never slept with any of the women I dated before Sam. But logic aside, the question was more disturbing than any before it, and worse yet, it begged an even more tortuous one: *How could I ever feel good about myself as a parent if I might have sired illegitimate kids I've unknowingly abandoned?* That whole prospect haunted me for weeks, maybe months. And now, three years later, I know it's coming back for me once more, like a playground bully who's been waiting at the fence.

By nightfall, I am locked in my den, mentally reviewing every date I can remember with every girl I ever went out with.

Play. Rewind. Play. Rewind.

Is it possible I could have got any of them pregnant? Maybe while sharing a hot tub, or simply locked in a passionate embrace? Reason is no longer a part of even my best thought-processing.

I think back on all the weird hang-ups I'd always

had about intimacy. Unlike most every college guy in America who was trying to get a woman into bed, I was doing all I could to ensure my dates never wound up there. I'd always spun it as a matter of morals. But, truth is, I couldn't imagine having sex with a woman who might get pregnant and might disappear from my life and might be carrying a child I'd never know about then. Talk about having to live with the ultimate uncertainty!

None of this ever struck me as odd until just now, as I sit here thinking about what great care my college-self had taken to protect me from the very hell I now find myself in.

On June first, three weeks to the day after first slithering into Dr. X's office building, I am about to slither out for the very last time.

He doesn't know this yet.

Our third session had passed quickly, and now this one is too. We've continued to talk about success, and why young professionals, in particular, have so much trouble dealing with it. I like the whole theory. As psychiatric hang-ups go, this seems like a noble one.

But I've been holding back, and I know it. Never once have I mentioned the tapes, or my bastard children concerns, or even my increasing troubles walking away from a car without going back to check its parking brake at least two or three times.

Now Dr. X is again peering over my shoulder, giving me the old let's-wrap-it-up-for-the-day smile. He's not saying anything, though, as he usually does at the end of our sessions.

"I guess this is it," I finally say.

"Is it?"

"Well, this *was* our fourth appointment, and I *am* doing much better."

"Are you?"

"Yeah. Wouldn't you say we're done with our work?"

"I don't know. What do you think?"

Enough with the damn questions, already. Is this what all shrinks do, throw everything back at you?

"Why don't you think about coming back for a while," he says after a second or two of silence.

"I'll give it some thought," I promise, knowing damn well that I've already made up my mind.

Thirty minutes later, I am back at Oyster Point Marina, making up for weeks worth of lost checking, and assessing the damage to my permanent record.

six

fast-forward 4 months

Samantha and I are on a Boeing 747, thirty seconds out of San Francisco International and headed for Honolulu. The plane is banking to the west, offering us and half the other passengers a perfect view of the shrinking peninsula below.

I can't look. I already made that mistake several months ago on a flight to Los Angeles. As I discovered the hard way that day, Oyster Point Marina sits just below the SFO flight path, and if you happen to be peering out a port-side window at takeoff, you can't help but see the goddamn cabin cruiser and its unmistakable blue tarp just as clear as can be.

I won't fall into that trap today.

I close my eyes and count to ten, then allow myself a quick peek. All the boats on the bay below are now just little toy figures. A few seconds later they are indistinguishable dots. If only I could do the same thing with the hellish vessels that drop anchor in my head—somehow make them disappear with nothing more than some time and distance.

Samantha's nose is buried in a book, so I close my eyes again and try to think about beaches and palm trees. Instead I see the very aerial image of the marina I was trying to avoid. It is still archived from my LA trip and redevelops like a Polaroid snapshot. Never mind all my efforts today; within minutes, I am again right back to thinking about that day, nearly a full year ago now, when my whole world began spiraling out of control. Right back to reviewing all of Doubt's *what-if?* questions about the fate of the surely doomed cabin cruiser. The scenarios make me shiver still, and with the conditioned response of Pavlov's dog, I replay my tape of the boat mishap for the billionth time, tears welling up in my eyes as I grasp for the illusory pause button. I know the best way, the only way, to stop one tape is to put on another. So I cue up the tape of my pathetic conversation with the guy from the cabin cruiser. Then I switch to the one of Nicole and me on the dock in the rain. Next up, a looped review of the time I inflated a small life raft and rowed it right by the cabin cruiser for a closer look at its bow. There are so many tapes in my growing collection.

Samantha leans over and tugs on my sleeve. "We're gonna have such a great time," she whispers with the excitement of a kid at Christmas. Sam is six months pregnant now and years overdue for the Hawaii vacation I've always promised her. She's all but giddy, flipping through the pages of an island guide, scribbling her planning notes in the margins.

II PAUSE You know that old pearl of parental wisdom, *Life isn't fair*? Like many parents, Samantha and I often find ourselves reminding our daughters of this. It's the perfect response, really, when one of them demands an explanation for why she has to, or isn't allowed to, do something or another.

Sometimes, though, when I watch Sam issue the admonishment with feigned seriousness—hands on hips, eyes narrowed to a squint—I can't help but wonder if the words sting with truth for her. Life *hasn't* been fair for my wife, at least not when it comes to getting what she bargained for with me.

For as long as I've known her, Samantha has displayed a rare mastery of the art of fun. No one else I've ever met can come close to squeezing as much sheer enjoyment from life. The quintessential kid at heart, she can spend hours playing board games, touring amusement parks, sledding in the snow, or roller skating. Dollar Scoop Tuesdays at Baskin-Robbins, those elusive packages of *fresh* gummy bears, hard-fought victories in her tanning show-downs with her mother: these are the things that make Sam crinkle her nose in delight. And then there's her favorite motto, the one shouting from the back of her most tattered T-shirt: "Life's uncertain. Eat dessert first."

Fans of TV's *Gilmore Girls* would recognize a whole lot of Lorelai in Samantha, especially the genuine playfulness and self-assuredness they share. I often think of that connection when remembering a fancy birthday dinner I'd taken Sam out for one year. "We can go anywhere you want when we're done," I'd told her over dessert. "Dancing. A movie. Jazz club. You name it."

It couldn't have been more than a few seconds before Sam's eyes lit up. "You know that super-slide at the fairgrounds?"

We were there ten minutes later.

Our courting days back in the mid-1980s played out well within my "normal years," and the guy Sam fell in love with was not only normal, but almost every bit as carefree and fun-loving as she was. After countless picnics and camping trips and moonlit strolls on the beach, who could blame Sam for thinking she'd found the perfect match for the rest of her fun-filled life?

Who could blame her for struggling to understand, years later on a plane to Hawaii, that *fun* was going to be a solo pursuit for the long stretch ahead?

And who could blame her if she began to find this marriage unfair?

Not me.

PLAY "So what do you think?"

Samantha is staring at me, waiting for a response, I'm guessing, to some question I've missed. This seems to happen a lot these days.

"What's that?" I say.

"Are you ignoring me again?"

"No, I was just—"

"Yeah, I know what you were doing," Sam says, tapping her finger on my head. "What I said was, 'This is your birthday trip—the big *three-oh*—remember? And you, my dear, have a lot to celebrate. Right?'"

She *is* right. So much has happened in the few short months since my wasted time and money with Dr. X. The good doctor may have failed to fix me, but all his talk about success must have, in some strange cosmic way, prompted that much more of it to come my direction. Just weeks after our final session, and years after first trying to get even a toe in the door at KCBS Radio, I got a call from the station's program director, Ed Cavagnaro, asking if I was still interested in working for him. A few weeks later I found myself broadcasting from the palatial Embarcadero Center studios of the CBS Network's West Coast flagship. And then within days, Cavagnaro called again to offer me double the work. Now I'm a regular weekend anchor and relief reporter at San Francisco's legendary all-news station, and KSFO seems like small potatoes.

Samantha's right. I do have a lot to celebrate. But then again, maybe old Dr. X was right as well—maybe I *am* afraid of my own success. All I know sitting here on this plane headed for Hawaii is that I'd trade my KCBS break and anything else in a heartbeat, just to ascertain once and for all what happened with the boats.

■

Settling into paradise proves to be no easy task. It's been years since Samantha and I have gotten away together, just the two of us. No parenting duties. No phone calls. No household chores. There is so much extra space to fill, so much extra time to play all my tapes.

Sam decides I need to keep busy, so we catch a

bus to Hanama Bay and rent snorkeling equipment. The water is perfect. The fish are beautiful. But my snorkel is old and battered, and ten minutes into our grand adventure, I realize that the mouthpiece is loose. *Did I do that? Break it somehow?* Soon my head is filled with visions of the next renter of this equipment choking on a mouthful of water. *What if that happens?* Doubt reminds me that *you'll never know for sure* and that *you'll spend the rest of your life worrying.* There's a virtual snorkeling tape in the making here, and I'm certain I'll be stuck watching it forever.

I tell Sam it's time to head back to the shore.

■

The next morning, we make plans to tour the other side of the island. A rental car offers the only efficient way to do this in one day. But I don't want to drive, and I find myself hemming and hawing. Samantha understands, even without my explaining. She knows I've lost all confidence in myself behind the wheel and she knows I'm scared to death that I might somehow screw up the car. *What if somebody else gets killed because I unknowingly broke something?*

Sam disappears into the rental car office.

"We're all set," she tells me a few minutes later. "But it turns out I'm the only one authorized to drive. That okay with you?" My wife is getting good at covering for me.

I tell her I guess so, dropping my head a bit in embarrassment. Why is it so humiliating for a guy to let his wife do the driving?

The day goes fine until we return our Ford Tempo in the late afternoon. While lifting our bags out of the trunk, I notice the left-rear wheel is missing its hubcap.

"Sam," I say, pointing toward the wheel.

"Yeah?"

"It's missing."

"What's missing?" My wife is confused.

"The hubcap! Was it there when we started out this morning?"

"I assume not," she says, without a hint of a care.

"Well, what if it fell off on our watch?"

"Are you serious?"

"Yeah."

"Don't you think we'd have heard something?"

"I dunno. What if it just came off?"

Sam narrows her eyes. "Okay," she says, "let's assume it came off. Not much we can do about it now."

My skin is growing cold, despite the tropical heat. I want to retrace our route, make sure that the hubcap hasn't become some hazard, lying like an unexploded land mine some place in the road.

Perhaps a guy on a motorcycle will hit it, sending him flying across the pavement and into a life as a paraplegic. There are so many possible horror scenarios. But as much as I want to go back for a look, it's simply not an option, so instead I focus on the Tempo.

"Maybe there's a safety issue," I say.

"For the Tempo?"

"I dunno." Logic is not a factor here.

Sam has closed her eyes. She doesn't know what to say to me. Pregnancy has made her somewhat less patient with all my challenges and quirks.

I break the silence seconds later, conveying the message that Doubt is whispering in my head: "We've got to tell the rental office that the hubcap is missing."

"I'm sure they already know," Sam says, "or they will know, when they look it over."

"You're not hearing me," I say. "We have *got* to say something to the gal behind the counter. I am not going to spend the rest of my vacation wondering whether they know."

I am learning the game. Handle this now or pay the price later with hours of blurry playbacks. I can't explain this to Samantha, but I can and do again beg her to mention the hubcap when returning our keys. I know if I get involved in the dialogue, I'll blow things even further out of proportion, so I stand off in a corner of the rental office and watch the confused clerk ask Sam again what she's talking about. A hubcap? *Oooh*-kay.

■

Samantha is still frustrated with me the following morning. I am ruining our vacation. But today is October 21, so she has no choice but to be nice to me. It's my thirtieth birthday.

We spend the day at Waikiki Beach. Sam suggests I rent a sailboard and play in the waves, like I used to in our college years. But somehow after the whole rental car ordeal, we both know that's not such a great idea. Instead I get a small raft and join the throngs of tourists bobbing like driftwood in the shallow surf.

Samantha strips down to her maternity swimsuit and stakes out a spot on the beach just in front of me. Within minutes, her eyes are closed. She looks so peaceful. Six months pregnant with a belly the size a basketball, yet she couldn't appear any more comfortable, any more at peace. I wonder what that must be like, to relax that way. It's been so long, I can't remember.

A nearby couple are in stitches about something, giggling so hard they wind up gasping for breath. They're doing this in front of me on purpose, I decide. Just to show off. Just to rub it in.

There must be two hundred people around me,

all of them showing off how much fun they can have, all of them rubbing it in. This is Hawaii, for God's sake. How can you not have fun? I close my eyes and try to think happy thoughts. I can't find any. Only looping clips of everything I've ever done wrong in my first three decades on earth. I try instead to think about the future, but for some reason, it's not there anymore. After years of conjuring up vivid images of my big career in radio, and my house in Tiburon overlooking the Bay, and my precocious kids' first piano recitals, I simply cannot put myself into a scene from the future.

I shiver the full length of my life raft, wondering just what this new development means.

■

"A tropical Mai Tai greeting. Scrumptious roasted pig, fresh from the imu. Songs and dances of Polynesia—"

Samantha is rattling off a list of the treats we're in for at Paradise Cove. We are headed there for an authentic Hawaiian luau, Sam's plan for the perfect culmination of my thirtieth birthday celebration. The bus trip is long and winding, and by the time we arrive, my stomach hurts as much as my head has for days.

The place is breathtaking. With its lush greenery and coconut palms, there's no question whatsoever that Paradise Cove is worthy of its name. It strikes me, in fact, that every Hawaiian postcard I've ever seen must have been shot on these grounds.

We make our way to the arts and crafts booths and the various game areas. Sam is like a kid taking her first lap around Disneyland. There is so much to do. She wants to take it all in.

"Hey, you want to try the spear throw?" Sam asks me, and I wonder if she's making a joke.

I tell her there ain't a chance in hell that I'm going to pick up that spear and send it flying through a crowd. I can't even walk through a shopping mall without inflicting damage. But it's too late. Some Polynesian stud with bulging muscles and a string of bones around his neck has appeared out of nowhere and is handing me a spear. I have no choice but to throw it, so I do. It lands safely on the grass. As near as I can tell, no one has died—though I myself am suddenly feeling gravely ill. Our island host retrieves the spear and suggests I try again. I shake my head no, and send him on his way.

"Ooops," Sam says, scrunching up her face. "Sorry 'bout that. What do you say we just go make a bead necklace for Nicole?"

I dunno. My stomach is all messed up now, and I can't be sure I'm not coming down with some bug. I probably shouldn't go putting my paws in that big vat of beads. *What if somebody else gets my germs and gets sick?*

I tell Sam that she should go have some fun without me. She says that's ridiculous, that she wants to spend my birthday with me. So the two of us stand around for the next several hours—stand around and do nothing, because I'm afraid to string beads. And afraid to throw a spear. And afraid to rent a sailboard. And afraid to drive a rental car. And afraid to use a snorkel. And afraid to look out my plane window.

Just plain afraid.

Soon the sun is setting and Samantha and I are standing on a beach at the edge of the luau grounds. The sky is a thousand shades of yellow and orange.

"I'm so sorry," Sam whispers. "I really thought you'd enjoy all this."

"I am," I say, but the lie just hangs there in the air between us. We stand in silence for a good five minutes, watching this huge ball of brilliant golden light sink slowly into the Pacific.

The sun setting on Paradise. What a prophetic moment this would prove to be.

seven

fast-forward 5 months

And baby makes four.

Brianna is ten weeks old now. Samantha is back at work part-time. Nicole is adjusting to life as a big sister. And I am trying like hell to be a contributing member of my family.

Never before has Sam needed me more; no longer can she carry our whole team on her own. I want to be there for her. I want to be a husband and father. I want to help shape the life of this precious little creature, who from the first moment I saw her has reminded me that I *am* still capable of doing something right, even if that something is merely passing along my chromosomes.

Today Sam needs me to pick up Nicole from daycare and watch her for a few hours. I've promised to oblige, so when my shift at Channel 2 wraps up I rush off to my car and head for Crayon College in San Bruno, where Nikki is waiting for me.

The traffic leaving Oakland is stacked up even more than usual this morning. Road crews are working on the Jackson Street on-ramp to northbound 880, doing earthquake retrofitting, I think. I hate construction zones. All those workers milling around within inches of my passing car. More and more, I catch myself worrying that I might clip some guy in a hard hat and not even realize it. Thank God for rearview mirrors, although they too have their limitations.

Now I see what's going on. A series of orange road cones, the narrow tubular kind, is squeezing two lanes into one in the thirty feet or so before the on-ramp. Crap. These merges are the worst. I want to find an alternate route, but it's too late. I am sandwiched between cars to the front, rear, and side of me.

I get lucky; the merge goes smoothly. As for the construction workers, it turns out they are well off the road, safely away from me.

I let out a sigh of relief, but it turns into a gasp

of panic as I watch an orange road cone pop up from under the right rear tire of the car just in front of me.

I'm no more than five feet away from it now, and closing in quickly. Four feet. Three feet. Two. The cone disappears, only to pop up in my rearview mirror a second later, then vanish again beneath the car behind me.

My pulse and blood pressure go through the roof. I want to pull my car over, but I'm on the on-ramp now and there's very little room. I check the mirror again and see one car after another knock over the beleaguered road cone. Like one of those old Weeble toys—the ones that "wobble but they don't fall down"—the damn thing just keeps popping back up.

I'm on 880 before I know it. The cone disappears from my line of sight. The Broadway exit is coming up, and I tell myself I should take it so I can loop around to Jackson and have another look at the cone. I've been doing this a lot lately—retracing my route when I'm behind the wheel. Just to make sure that potholes and street bumps aren't really pedestrians I've hit, and that car honks and sirens aren't the results of anything I've done. Sometimes a single loop will make me feel better, sometimes it takes two or three. But I haven't got time to loop back even once now. Nicole is waiting for me.

I try coaching myself as I make my way across

the Bay Bridge. Clearly I was not the only vehicle—or even the first—to run over this cone. Hell, I watched the car in front of me do the very same thing.

Or did I?

Right on cue, Doubt checks in to make sure I question my rational conclusions. *Perhaps you just imagined seeing the cone emerge from under that car ahead of you. Maybe* you *knocked it over first.*

My physical senses, I am finding, are growing almost irrelevant in my day-to-day life.

The Treasure Island exit is coming up. I could turn off and go back to Jackson Street and still make it to Crayon College no more than twenty minutes late. That would be entirely forgivable. But a bus keeps me from getting over to the exit in time. I tell myself I can wait until tomorrow morning after work to check things out.

The trip through San Francisco is painfully slow. My head is throbbing again. I need to see the flattened cone, figure out its position relative to traffic and everything else. I think back on all the sleep I lost over the boat incident in those early days and realize I'm never going to rest tonight if I don't go sort out everything in Oakland this afternoon.

Nicole and I will just have to take a little field trip.

12:00 noon. The morning session at Crayon College is letting out. Vulnerable little kids are running around everywhere. If there's one thing I hate even more than construction zones, it's a parking lot full of toddlers and minivans.

Nicole is thrilled to see me. Several weeks ago she turned three, and suddenly she seems so grown up. So much more plugged in to what's going on in her world. I know I have to be more careful now in covering my tracks around her. So when she asks me if we can go to the park, I'm quick on my feet.

"I've got a much better idea, honey," I tell her.

"Really?!" Nicole's eyes light up. Her smile brightens.

"How 'bout you and I go for a walk."

"Where?" she wants to know.

"In a really special, secret place."

Nicole loves adventures. The more mysterious the better.

"Cool!"

My older daughter can't wait to see what I have in store for her this afternoon.

12:50 p.m. The trip back to Oakland took a good forty minutes, enough time to boost Nicole's excitement about my plans for the two of us. She looks perplexed as I pull our car up to a metered spot beneath the freeway at the Jackson Street on-ramp, and so too does an obviously drunk, unkempt man in his fifties who watches us park.

"We're here!" I say with feigned excitement.

"*This* is where we're going to walk?" Nicole's enthusiasm is gone in a heartbeat.

I explain that there's a really cool construction zone just around the corner and that the two of us are going to check it out.

"*Oooh*-kay." Nikki decides to give me the benefit of the doubt.

The sidewalk is torn up, but I need to get closer, so I walk my frightened daughter along the gutter. Cars whiz by, inches from the two of us. Nicole turns to look at me. I tell her everything is fine.

I find a spot on the corner just across from the on-ramp, maybe ten feet from my orange cone, whose base I now note is somehow affixed to the concrete. Car after car knocks it over as it tries to spring upright time and again. I see that the cone is set well into the lane and right in the path of traffic. It would be damn near impossible to avoid running over it.

Perhaps, indeed, everything *is* in order.

"Daddy?" Nicole is tugging on my sleeve. "I don't get why we're here." She's grown up so much since our last covert mission.

I try explaining that I wanted to show her how a construction crew works, but I can tell she's not buying my act.

"You're right," I say. "I guess this isn't really all that interesting. Let's just go home."

2:30 p.m. Nicole is playing with her dolls in the living room, and Samantha arrives home with Brianna. She finds me sitting on the stairs, hunched over and stretching my hair back across the top of my head.

Sam puts Bri in her jumper and walks over to me. "What happened?" she asks. "You look awful. Is everything okay?"

"I'm fine," I say. But I am not, and Sam knows it.

"Talk to me, Jeff."

"I can't." I know if I try now, I'm going to break apart into a thousand pieces.

Sam puts her arms around me, feels me shaking. I pray to God Nicole won't come walking into the hallway.

"Tell me what happened," my wife begs of me.

I start to cry, slowly at first, but uncontrollably within seconds. I do my best to recount my morning, in all its gory detail.

Sam assures me that everything's fine. I shake my head, tell her I need to go back to Oakland.

"Why?" she asks. "I don't understand."

"I've got to talk to the road crew."

"And tell them what?" Sam is trying so hard to tap into my thinking.

"That one of their cones is in the wrong place and keeps getting run over."

"I must be missing something," she decides. "I honestly don't get why that's *your* responsibility."

Because that's how it feels, I want to tell her.

Because Doubt is whispering that I've got no other choice—except, that is, to keep reviewing the whole thing in my mind until I can rule out all the potential consequences and my own culpability.

"It's just easier this way," I say under my breath, as I grab my coat and car keys and head for the door.

4:00 p.m. *Where the hell are they?* I am looking everywhere at the Jackson Street construction site for *someone* I can tell about the misplaced road cone. It appears the workers have gone home for the day. But after another forty-five minutes of sitting in trans-Bay traffic, I am unwilling to accept this unexpected development. Damn these guys for making me wait until the morning to share my concerns. I can now add anger to the mix of emotions tearing me to shreds.

By the time I'm back on the Bay Bridge for my *sixth* trip of the day across the span, traffic is in full rush-hour mode. Bumper to bumper. Crawling along the upper deck at three miles an hour now, I find myself staring off to the west at the four jutting towers of the Embarcadero Center, wishing I had a reason to be there tonight. With each passing week, KCBS has become more of a safe haven for me. Behind the microphone, I am king of the world, even more so than I was at KSFO. I live for my on-air hours every week, for that rare sense of pride I always manage to find in them.

Anchoring the news is the one thing in my life I can still do with any confidence. Yet, sitting here now thinking back on recent shifts, I realize that even at KCBS, I have started hedging my bets. After years of rolling tape on my air shifts, more out of habit than anything else, I now find myself playing back my cassette airchecks all too often, listening for something or another I may have said or failed to say. So important have these damn tapes become to me that I recently snapped at an assistant editor who turned off a machine airchecking my show. "Sorry, just an old quirk of mine," I explained when he asked why, unlike any other anchor in the building, I see this need to record everything I do on the air.

6:00 p.m. Samantha is waiting for me at the door. She's been worried, she says, wondering why I've been gone so long. Dinner is getting cold. She wants me to eat.

I tell her I'm not hungry and disappear into the downstairs bathroom. As the door closes behind me, I let it all out. Tears. Screams. Sixteen months' worth of pent-up rage. I simply cannot stand the pain anymore.

Soon I am curled up next to the toilet on a cold tile floor, the very one on which I found myself a full year ago during Nicole's second birthday party. From my vantage point down here, the world is spinning with the fury of a Midwest tornado. I am a mere passenger, spiraling without hope into a violent vortex.

Suddenly an arm reaches out and saves me from my fall.

Samantha, it seems, has laid herself down next to me and is burrowing her head into my upper back.

"It's okay," she whispers, "Everything is going to be okay." My wife is speaking in the same hushed tones she uses with baby Brianna in the middle of the night.

"I—don't—know—what—is—hap—pen—ing—to—me." My words come out as single syllables between gasps for air.

"You need help, Jeffie. We're going to find you help."

I turn around and see that I'm not the only one crying.

12:00 midnight. A piercing horn sounds just in front of me. It's coming from the car I'm about to slam into. I throw my head back and it hits something soft. My pillow. I am in my bed. The car crash is a dream. The horn is my alarm. Another nightmare about crashing vehicles. This is the rest I get when I finally close my eyes for five or six hours every night.

It's time to get up now. I need to be at work in an hour.

9:01 a.m. The closing credits are still rolling as I bee-line it out the door at Channel 2. My eight-hour shift has felt double that long. I've been counting the minutes until I can get out of here and over to Jackson Street. No major writing mistakes overnight. But, then again, not much of anything has come out of my worthless word processor.

I hear myself whisper *Thank God* as I pull up to the construction site and see a crew back at work on the on-ramp. My punching bag road cone is still taking its hits.

I park my car and make my way over to the workers. A fence stands between me and the five of them, so I wave my arms and try to get someone's attention. Finally, a guy in a hard hat sees me and puts down his jackhammer. He takes a few steps toward the fence and cups a hand behind his ear.

"Your road cone," I shout, pointing back toward the street.

"Huh? Can't hear you," says this big burly man. He motions me to hang on and walks right up to the fence.

"I ran over your road cone," I say, again point-ing at the nearly flattened cone bobbing between passing car tires.

He gives me a blank look, one of those to which I'm becoming all too accustomed. "That thing?"

"Yeah, I just wanted to make sure you knew about that downed cone."

Again a blank stare.

"Thanks," he says at last. "I'll pass along word to the foreman."

With his words, I am instantly better. The fear. The anxiety. The guilt. The uncertainty. Gone in an instant, all of them.

Sam is wrong; I don't need to get help. I've learned how to solve my problems all by myself. So what if my approach costs me every last bit of my dignity?

eight

fast-forward 3 weeks

"And how does that make you *feel?*"

Dr. Y looks troubled as she poses the question to me. Her brow is furrowed, the corners of her mouth are turned down, and she's leaning so far forward in her chair that I'm afraid she'll fall out. We've known each other less than thirty minutes, yet clearly she's far more concerned about my feelings than even my oldest and dearest of friends.

"Okay, let's back up," she says in response to my silence. "These persistent thoughts of yours, let's talk about them."

"Well, they're always about harm," I tell her,

"harm I may have caused in the past, or harm I may yet cause in the future, always some form of harm stemming from my negligence."

"Good. And that makes you feeeel . . ." She wants me to fill in the blank.

"Guilty, I guess."

"Good! Very good." Her frown is a smile now, but an awkward, askew, and generally unnatural one. "Okay," she says. "Now tell me more about your childhood *situation*."

It's a late April morning, and I am back in a psychologist's office. It turns out Samantha was right after all: I *can't* seem to tackle my problems alone. Just two days after my road-cone troubles in Oakland, there I was on my hands and knees in San Bruno, combing our street for fragments of a flashlight battery I'd run over with my car, determined to make sure that no children could be exposed to any sharp or poisonous parts. Then, three days after that, I got so worked up over a tough lane change that I almost didn't make it to my reporting shift at KCBS. Sam and I later had a big, ugly argument over nothing, prompting me to storm out of the house. After several hours of stewing in my parked car, I came to understand that perhaps she'd been right all along.

And now here I am in the sterile offices of Dr. Y, whose only qualifications I'm familiar with are the ones she listed in the Yellow Pages. Truth is, she had me at the first line that established her gender. Somehow talking with a middle-aged man had been a bit too much like talking with Dad. This time, I was determined to find a female therapist.

At 9:50 we wrap up our session and make arrangements to meet every Monday. Dr. Y's frown is back as I get up to leave. It strikes me that there's no rhyme or reason behind the expressions she straps on her face. Her last words to me on my way out the door: "I want you to think this week about how you are feeling."

What I am *feeling* by the time I get home is an overwhelming urge to visit Oyster Point Marina. Several months ago, Dad decided to move The Boat across the Bay to Alameda, and at first it seemed the new berthing arrangement would solve all my problems. No longer would I have to see the cabin cruiser every time I went to the boat. But then the notion crossed my mind that I was somehow leaving the scene of a crime, and with each passing week, Doubt's hit-and-run prosecution has grown that much stronger. Now, the damning evidence tapes again loop in my head daily, and I've come to realize that the only way to exonerate myself is to spell out everything in writing for the crew of the cabin cruiser.

When Samantha comes home, I tell her about my big plans.

"You want to leave them a note?" she says. "And just what will that accomplish?"

"It'll let me know they can reach me if they need to," I tell her, knowing at some deeper level that what I'm really hoping for is another rush of relief like I got when I confessed my road-cone concerns to the construction crew foreman.

"You know this isn't about the boat anymore," Sam says, "if in fact it ever was."

I say nothing.

"The road cone. The hubcap in Hawaii. That . . . that old battery you were wigging out over. It's something new every day, babe. You do see that, don't you?"

"But if I can just leave this note—"

Sam closes her eyes for a second, then leaves to put Bri down for her nap.

■

The following Monday, I tell Dr. Y about the note Samantha couldn't keep me from slipping into the cockpit of the cabin cruiser. She narrows her eyes and asks me to describe my feelings about it.

The Monday after that, I recount a recent afternoon I spent looping my car around downtown San Francisco, looking for the object that had made such a clang beneath my wheels—looking *in person,*

I explain, so I won't later have to do it in my mind for hours on end.

"Let's back up to that noise," she says. "How did you feel when you first heard the clang?"

We do this dance for fifty minutes every Monday for the next two months. In between discussions about my feelings, I answer Dr. Y's many questions about my youth: Did my parents ever argue? Yes? Oh, how often then? Did I blame myself when there was tension between them? Did I ever experience a sense of helplessness when times weren't good? Like Dr. X, Dr. Y takes copious notes, though she tends to pontificate far less than he did. Still, every now and then, she stops me midsentence and offers an observation.

"It's interesting," she tells me one day after listening to my concern about having bumped into somebody at the station. "You seem to have a very inflated sense of your own power."

No argument there, I think to myself. When it comes to harming people, I *know* I've got incredible power—Herculean, in fact. I can inflict brain damage with the slightest touch, and impregnate women without even undressing.

You nailed that one, Doc, I want to throw back at her.

By late June, I have spent ten hours and a thousand dollars with Dr. Y. I don't feel any better. Don't seem to have anything to show for my investments. But therapy is a slow process, she tells me again and again, so I resolve to keep my Monday appointments. I'll hang in there for Samantha's sake, if nothing else.

II PAUSE I sometimes think my memory has been a bit unfair to good ol' Dr. Y. She is, in my tapes, nothing short of a cartoon caricature, a stereotype reflecting every grudge I long held against traditional psychotherapists and their once widespread ignorance of my particular brand of crazy. The endless questions. The constant probing for some elusive defining moment or event that, once identified, would unlock all my secrets. Take my various quirks, for example: the driving in loops, the urges to confess, the repeated checking and rechecking of everything around me, even my constant mental reviews—they, Dr. Y assured me, were all indications of a much deeper, broader, and far more complex problem. Our challenge in therapy, she explained, was to root out that problem. Clearly this approach is an effective one in treating many kinds of issues. But not mine. Today I'm convinced of this; but even back then, sitting on Dr. Y's couch week after week, I knew it also, if only in my gut. I knew she was missing something, and I count my blessings to this day that the checker, and the investigative reporter, in me just wouldn't let it go.

It's late August now, and Dr. Y is away, **PLAY** wrapping up a three-week vacation. I, on the other hand, am very much on the job, tackling an investigative research project with all the discipline and fervor that, several years ago, had landed me a big award from the Associated Press.

I am camped out in the psychology section of the Oakland Barnes & Noble—probably not such a great idea given its close proximity to the Channel 2 studios. But even this is a risk I'm willing to take to get to the bottom of the story I'm working on—*my* story, the one Dr. Y can't seem to sort out.

As I discover right away, bold-lettered subcategories such as "Tape Reviews" or "Confession Urges" or even "Driving Issues" simply don't exist, so I start at the upper left shelf in the General Psychology area and begin making my way down and across the alphabetical series. For forty-five minutes I scan each and every title, taking an occasional book off the shelf when its title mentions guilt or uncertainty or even general anxiety. But nothing fits. I am not recovering from a broken marriage or grieving over a lost loved one. I am not a victim of child abuse or fighting urges to take my own life. I am, I decide, a true freak of nature battling mental problems beyond the scope of any psychology or self-help book on the market. Perhaps my little research project wasn't such a brilliant plan after all.

It's getting late and I've nearly exhausted my third bank of books when a bright orange one with the strangest of titles catches my eye. *The Boy Who Couldn't Stop Washing.* Something about the words *couldn't stop* prompts me to pull the small paperback off the shelf. What I read on the first page of the first chapter knocks me down to my knees, like a swift blow to the back of my legs.

I lose myself in this book for the next five—or is it fifty?—minutes, slowly processing the firsthand account of someone named Dr. S describing an auto accident that never was. Using words that could very well be my own, this thirty-six-year-old Ph.D. explains how he's driving down the highway one day when, for no logical reason, the thought crosses his mind that maybe he's hit someone. He knows it's a ridiculous thought, but he also knows the price he'll later pay for not checking on it. So he turns his car around and goes back for a look. He checks the side of the road, finds no evidence, and now, greatly relieved, drives off again. Twenty seconds later, though, he's kicking himself for not inspecting the brush alongside the road. So he heads back once more, and things go from bad to worse as he checks and rechecks the shoulder again and . . .

I am starting to break down now. And I don't care. Let the whole damn Channel 2 news department show up and see me like this. I just don't care. Sure, grown men aren't supposed to cry, certainly not while sitting on the floor of a busy bookstore. But grown men also aren't supposed to drive their cars in circles and battle nonsensical thoughts about harming other people. Discovering, as I just have, that at least one other grown man in this world does these things too: that is reason enough to let it all out.

Still, there is much more to read. I force myself to push on to a story about a nine-year-old named Zach who can't stop washing his hands, and a thirteen-year-old named Arnie who has to mentally review every event of his day.

A kid who plays tapes!

Dr. S and Zach and Arnie and the dozen or so other men, women, and children profiled in the little orange book all have one thing in common, according to its author, Dr. Judith Rapoport: they all battle a "strange and fascinating sickness of ritual and doubts run wild." Obsessive-compulsive disorder, she calls it. OCD.

I have all but finished reading the book by the time I take it to the cashier and make it my own.

At home two hours later Samantha sees my red eyes and assumes I've been spending more time on a cold bathroom floor. I shake my head and silently hand her my copy of *The Boy Who Couldn't Stop Washing*. I watch her troubled face as she reads the pages I've bookmarked and see in her expressions a reflection of my own witch's brew of emotions. The confusion. The disbelief. The fear. The hope and the cautious optimism.

"Yeah?" I whisper after a few seconds of silence.

"Yeah," she says. "No question about it."

Dr. Y is somewhat less convinced.

"O-C what?" she says after I spend the first fifteen minutes of our session running through the highlights of my life-changing discovery at Barnes & Noble just the day before.

"OCD," I repeat. "Obsessive-compulsive disorder."

"And you read about this in a book while I was on vacation?"

"Yeah, I've gone through it twice now, and the case studies are so similar to my own experiences, it's downright eerie."

Dr. Y bites her lip, then shakes her head, an inch to the left and an inch to the right. She is weighing her words as that awkward smile of hers reappears. *Jeff, Jeff, Jeff,* I know she wants to say. *Patients really shouldn't try to do the work of a trained psychologist.*

"I'm very committed to exploring this whole OCD label," I tell her when I can't wait a second longer for her thoughts.

"I can see that," she says. "I'm just concerned that you're losing sight of the underlying problems."

We stare at each other in silence for what seems like forever. And then I make a decision, one I'm not sure I even saw coming when I stepped into her office this morning.

"I think it's time for me to move on, Dr. Y," I announce. "I do hope you understand."

Damn, that felt good, I think on my way to the door. How ironic that the one time I'd really like to share my *feelings,* I know I can't because of how hurtful they'd be.

■

Over the next twenty-four hours, I hole up and read every book on obsessive-compulsive disorder that I can find in the library. With titles like *When Once Is Not Enough* and *Over and Over Again,* the books are all so strangely familiar. On their pages I uncover the harsh realities of who and what I am.

The vocabulary comes first, with familiar words taking on whole new meanings that hit close to home. *Obsessions,* for example. They are, in the lexicon of my new world, *intrusive, nonsensical thoughts that produce great distress.* And *compulsions*: they are now and forever more *repetitive, hard-to-resist actions or rituals that temporarily reduce this distress.*

Other words, too, keep appearing, seemingly with my picture next to their every definition. One of these is *checker,* which I learn is an obsessive-compulsive whose obsessions tend to involve catastrophic *what-if?* questions, and whose compulsions entail various forms of physical and mental checking aimed at warding off the imagined catastrophes.

Slowly, everything starts to come together, like a jigsaw puzzle taking form from a box full of jagged pieces of myriad sizes, colors, and shapes. Doubt's nagging and disturbing questions of me—*What if the cabin cruiser sinks? What if the road cone causes an accident? What if you inflicted brain damage on that kid you bumped into?*—these are all uncertainty-riddled *obsessions* that fill me with anxiety. And my relentless "tape reviews," along with the physical inspections and driving loops and repeated confessions—these are all *checking compulsions* I've adopted in a futile effort to remove the unbearable doubt of these obsessions and make them disappear forever.

Symptoms of a larger problem, Dr. Y? Hmmm. What if maybe the symptoms are *the problem*?!

From my research I learn that as many as three out of every 100 Americans are believed to be battling this so-called "doubting disease." But as OCD experts Edna Foa and Reid Wilson explain in their book *Stop Obsessing!* not all of them are *checkers* like myself. Some are *washers and cleaners,* consumed with obsessions about contamination. Others are *repeaters,* compelled to repeat certain actions. Still others are *orderers* who require that things around them be arranged in a particular, rigid way. Or *hoarders* who collect trivial objects and find it impossible to let them go. Or *thinking ritualizers* who mentally repeat thoughts or images. Or *worriers and pure obsessionals* who remain locked in repetitious negative thoughts.

Lots of different ways to make an omelet, with lots of different cracked eggs in the pan.

Soon I know enough to write a master's thesis on the mechanics of OCD and analyze in great detail all of Doubt's cruel games of mental keep-away. But what I can't do, even after countless hours of my best investigative reporting, is answer my most pressing question: *Why?* Why in God's name do I and the millions of other obsessive-compulsives out there do what we do?

Unfortunately, it seems no one really knows for sure.

Could be abnormalities in my brain's frontal

lobe and/or a portion of the basal ganglia known as the caudate nucleus, according to one book. Could be faulty neurotransmitters, such as serotonin, according to another. The only thing they all appear to agree on is that there's at least some biological explanation for the way an OC's thoughts "get stuck" in the transmission process, as evidenced by PET scans and other forms of high-tech brain imaging.

In the absence of cold, hard facts, good investigative reporters look for points of consensus. I find several in my stacks of books: (1) OCD is a chronic anxiety disorder that tends to kick in for most sufferers in early adulthood; (2) Adult OCD is often preceded by childhood symptoms that disappear during adolescent years, in a pattern very much like my own; (3) While OCD's roots are most likely (at least in part) biological, certain childhood environments (including those marked by parental perfectionism!) may tend to trigger the disorder in children already predisposed to develop its patterns; and (4) There's absolutely no evidence to suggest that OCD is indicative of any other larger neuroses. In fact, OCD sufferers are acutely and painfully aware of how irrational their thoughts and actions are, unlike people with delusions or other more serious problems.

As for OCD treatment options, it seems they are

every bit as varied as the theories regarding the disorder's cause. I shudder to read that until the 1950s, lobotomies were routinely performed in severe cases, and that in the decades that followed, hospitalization was common. My head fills with visions of mad scientists strapping me to a bed so they can take their scalpels to my frontal lobes. Fortunately, I read on to learn that today's treatment alternatives are significantly less severe and tend to fall into two often overlapping approaches: (1) *cognitive behavioral therapy,* in which OCs learn to confront their obsessive thoughts and curb their compulsive reactions to them, and (2) drug treatment, in which various psychopharmaceuticals are used to alter the neurotransmission process.

I know I'll never, under any circumstances, allow myself to be drugged. (I can't trust myself now; how could I have any confidence at all in my judgment while spaced out on pills?) But this cognitive therapy: how bad could it be? With eyes bloodshot from hours of reading and a head throbbing from far too much information processing, I decide to make a phone call and find out.

"O-C Foundation. How can I help you?"

"Yes. Right. Thank you. I . . . uh . . . I've been doing some reading, and I . . . well, I'm not sure, but I . . ."

The woman taking my call in Connecticut listens patiently, then, with a warmth in her voice that puts me at ease right away, asks what she can do.

"I . . uh . . . guess I need someone to point me in the right direction," I say.

"Well, you've come to the right place," my new best friend in the world tells me, then proceeds to suggest a number of resources right here in the Bay Area.

By the time we hang up, I have a name and number for a local OCD specialist at UC San Francisco who might be able to take on another client. Her name is Dr. Jacqueline Persons, and two phone connections later, I have an appointment to meet her at her office in Oakland.

Dr. Y calls me at home the following morning.

"Have you got a minute?" she asks.

"Uh, yeah, sure." In four months of working together, never once have we spoken outside of her office.

"I've been talking to a few colleagues, and, well, they seem to think there might be something to your theory."

"Really?" I say, trying my hardest not to sound like a smart-ass. I can only imagine how difficult it must have been for her to pick up the phone.

"Yeah. Anyway, I just thought you should know."

No award from the Associated Press could ever mean more to me than this particular recognition of my investigative reporting.

nine

fast-forward 1 day

I have my little speech all rehearsed and ready to go.

"Thank you for seeing me so soon, *Jackie*," I say, making sure she notices my deliberate use of her first name only. I've had it with therapist power-plays, and after researching Dr. Jacqueline Persons's long list of academic and professional credentials, I'm not about to take any chances this time around. My first words to her are a carefully launched trial balloon which, to my great relief, she chooses not to shoot down.

"You sounded pretty stressed on the phone," she says without even a hint of offense taken over my lack of formality. "Hopefully, we can get right to work."

"I'd like that. But first there's something I've got to put on the table."

"Go for it."

Jackie has a smile on her face, a playful, almost impish one that seems to tease, *I know exactly what you're going to tell me next.*

"Listen," I say, "You need to understand that I have no interest in telling you about my childhood."

"Really?"

"Really."

"Good, because I have no interest in hearing about it."

Jackie is looking right into my eyes, showing me, I think, that she is serious about this. Her expression is oddly familiar, much like one of Samantha's when I'm trying to test her and get caught in the act. Something less tangible, but just as pronounced, also reminds me of Sam: She has that same down-to-earth, Real McCoy, This-is-who-I-am-take-it-or-leave-it ease about her, and I can just tell she shares Sam's commitment to living life to its fullest. The rest of her story I can only guess: Early forties, probably. Earthy but sophisticated, with her long jet-black hair and stylish yet understated clothes. Could be an art dealer, if I didn't know otherwise. Married, judging by the ring. A mother of a young kid, based on a few office decorations.

"I'm a behavior therapist," Jackie says, her eyes still locked on mine. "As such, I'm far less concerned about *how* you came by your problems than I am about helping you *do something* about them."

I like this. I like her. I think I can shelve the rest of my speech.

We spend the next forty-five minutes talking about my various challenges and about the nuts and bolts of cognitive behavioral therapy. "This isn't going to be much fun," Jackie tells me, and I learn she's not kidding when she describes the mechanics of something called *exposure/response prevention,* a form of calculated torture—she refers to it as therapy—in which an obsessive-compulsive is exposed to a high-anxiety trigger and then prevented from responding to it with typical compulsions.

"Take your driving issues," Jackie says. "We may have you run over some loose manhole covers, then keep you from going back for a look."

"And you're going to charge me for this horror?"

"You bet," she says, with a disarming smile.

The idea, Jackie explains, is to desensitize me to my obsessive fears and help me break my compulsive habits, like driving in circles and checking everything around me, even reviewing things in my head again and again.

"This is hard work, Jeff," she tells me for the third or fourth time. "That's why a lot of my patients choose to go on medication to help take off the edge."

And there it is. The other shoe falling. Right on cue. Right on top of me. Splat. I am trapped in my chair now, feeling the pressure, wanting like hell to bolt from her office.

Jackie recites a string of reasons to try meds, reasons I'm now quite familiar with from my OCD research. She pauses and looks up at me, seeming to have no problem translating my body language. "Listen," she says, "it's *entirely* your choice. I'm just saying I think you should consider it."

"Not a chance," I tell her. I've seen *One Flew Over the Cuckoo's Nest.* No way am I going to let myself become some drugged-out vegetable, standing in line for my daily Dixie cup of assorted tablets, dependent on chemical compounds to get me through my day. Besides, psychiatric pills are for the serious nutcases. *Does she really think I'm one of them?*

An hour and ten minutes after starting our session, I notice that we've exceeded our scheduled time by fifteen minutes.

"Aren't you supposed to kick me out?" I ask, recalling my sessions with Drs. X and Y that ended mid-sentence at the stroke of a clock.

"Yeah, probably, but you were on a roll."

All things considered, I like this woman, Jackie Persons.

"You up for coming back?" she asks.

"Yeah."

"And you're serious about doing the hard work?"

I tell her I am, but I know I'm just trying to sound brave.

■

On Tuesday morning, four days after my first meeting with Jackie and two days before my next scheduled one, the unthinkable happens: I lose sight of a pedestrian who is "in my care." It happens as I'm making a left turn at a busy intersection. A disheveled homeless guy steps into the crosswalk moments after my rear tires cross the second white line. I know this because I watch him in my rearview mirror, much as I watch every person on foot who winds up in front of, behind, or next to my car, all of whom are logically my direct responsibilities forever. But this guy just disappears. One second he's there, the next he's gone. I never get to verify that he has safely made it to the other curb. In at least a year of meticulous pedestrian tracking, never even once before have I lost sight of a single walker.

I slow my car to a crawl, check all my mirrors. But it's almost lunchtime and the sidewalks are packed. Picking this guy out of the sea of people I can see in every direction will never be possible. I loop around the block and find a parking spot. At least ten minutes have passed, though, and none of the vagrants I spot looks anything like the one I remember. I comb the whole area for signs of a medical response team. I scour the street and sidewalk for blood or other evidence of a deadly accident. I make my way back and forth across the crosswalk, pausing for the signal each time, trying to get a sense of the timing involved in crossing the street.

This is OCD, I try to tell myself. Surely I would have seen, heard, or felt something if I'd hit this guy.

Bullshit, Doubt counters. *How can you ever be certain?*

I ponder the question for the next thirty-six hours, a good many of which I spend hounding Samantha for reassurance. My poor wife. She was so encouraged, so hopeful after my first hour with Jackie. Now here we are back at square one, as I beg her to walk through all the *what-if?* scenarios. When Sam tells me for the last time that I've got to move on, I lock myself in my room and play back my virtual tape of the incident. I see my car moving into the intersection. I see the homeless guy stepping off the curb. I see the throng of frenzied business types. I see myself looking in the rearview mirror. But then the tape ends cold. So I rewind it once again, searching in desperation for images I might have missed. Nothing. So I rewind again. And again. And again.

Mental reviewing, Jackie called this whole compulsion of mine. As if slapping some clinical label on it could somehow help.

At Channel 2 Wednesday night, I come up with a plan. I will go through the news wires, looking for items about local hit-and-runs. I know such a crime would garner at least a few lines of copy; therefore, in the *absence* of any relevant stories, I can safely assume that my homeless guy simply vanished into thin air. A search of the afternoon Bay Area wires comes up empty. Nothing involving unexplained accidents or plowed-down pedestrians. That familiar rush of relief shoots through my body like blasts of hot air defrosting my every fear-frozen cell. But I should check the morning wires too, I decide, just to be sure. So I do, and seconds later, I discover a story slug that leaves me gasping for breath: "Body Found."

In a mad panic, I scan the nine lines of copy and learn that the unidentified body was discovered at about eight o'clock Tuesday night, at a curb not all that far from where I'd driven. The man, believed to be in his fifties, was wearing a shirt that was rolled up to his chest, as if the body had been dragged. According to a quote from the coroner's office, the body showed no signs of trauma but bore what appeared to be a fresh needle mark on one arm.

A map. I need a damn map. Need to measure how far the cited location is from my busy intersection. Damn it, just as I feared: less than a mile. Several blocks, according to my dog-eared Thomas Guide. Given this piece of evidence and the mere nine hours separating my driving scare and the body's discovery, I know I'm in trouble. If there'd ever been any chance that my fears were simply OCD obsessions, that prospect no longer exists. I am, I am certain, a cold-blooded killer.

Staring at the news copy in front of me, I notice there's a media contact number for reporters wanting more information—a listing for the local coroner's office.

There you go, Doubt suggests.

No! I will not stoop to this new low. I will not allow myself to call under the guise of doing a story on. . . .

Shit.

I jot down the seven digits.

■

"You're—you're kidding me—right?"

Dr. Jacqueline Persons is in stitches, all but slapping her knee and wiping tears from the corners of her eyes.

"I'm sorry," she says after seeing the shock on my face. "Go on. Please. Really. This is good."

I don't know what the hell to say now. I'm paying this woman more than a hundred bucks an hour and she's laughing at me? This should tick me off big time; but instead, somehow, it seems to put me at ease.

"Let me just make sure I'm following this one," Jackie says. "You lost a guy you were tracking in your rearview mirror, and nine hours later a junkie shows up in a gutter three blocks away, and now you're convinced you somehow did the guy in?"

"Well, yeah, I guess." It all sounds so stupid when she throws it back at me like this, and now I think I *get* what's she's doing here: trying to make me recognize the absurdity of what I'm telling her.

"You don't really believe you killed that guy?"

"I could have," I protest, still not ready to give up.

"Right. And his body bounced three blocks to a curb where it landed on a hypodermic needle and was then mysteriously dragged another few feet for good measure?"

"I don't know—"

"Jeff, this is O-C-D!"

Jackie is laughing again, and I try to join her. But it's tears that come out and shake my whole torso.

"So why the hell does this all feel so real?" I ask when I can finally string together a sentence.

"Ahh, *emotional reasoning*," Jackie says and goes on to explain it like this: My misfiring brain reacts to a nonsensical thought with a biochemical fear-response generally reserved in "normal" people for logical scares, like a bear attack or an impending train collision. Because this fear-response is, in fact, very real, it lends a certain credibility to whatever trigger I've associated with it. In simpler terms, it *feels* as if something horrible has happened, therefore my deductive reasoning concludes that something horrible *has* indeed happened.

Intellectually, this makes sense to me. But intellect is the bullied little brother of emotion. It counts for little in the throes of panic. Perhaps this is why I want nothing more in the world than to call the coroner's office when I walk out of here—this, despite understanding at some level just how disastrous that would be.

■

Five days later I am back in Jackie's office, hanging my head low as she asks how I'm doing with the whole Bouncing Body episode. I'm supposed to be reporting all my successes today, showing her how serious I am about tackling my OCD. Instead, I'm copping to a laundry list of checking activities: The trips back to the intersection and surrounding area. The daily inspections of my car, bumper to bumper. The countless checks of the news wires for follow-up stories. And, of course, the endless playbacks of my virtual tapes of the incident.

Jackie grabs a yellow legal pad from her desk, and I get nervous. Here we go, I think, with images of her two predecessors and all their note-taking coming to mind. But Jackie has other plans. She lists all the checking drills I've just described and asks me to name every other compulsive urge that I'm battling. Then she has me rate them on a scale of zero to 100, in terms of my perceived need to follow through on each. Soon we've got a list of fifteen items ranging from 30 to 80. Next, I'm supposed to pick three of these compulsions that I can promise I won't act on for at least another week.

I pledge: (1) not to confess to the police, (2) not to call the coroner, and (3) not to return to the busy intersection.

"Good," Jackie says. "Now we're going to take some of these other items and put limits on them."

By the time I leave Jackie's office, I've committed to a whole series of daily caps: three discussions with Samantha about the incident, twelve checks of the Channel 2 wires for "body" stories, one bumper-to-bumper car inspection, and two five-minute stretches of mental reviewing.

■

This is just OCD.

But what if it's not?

Jackie's voice and Doubt's are battling it out in

my head as I try in vain to hide from them both. It's mid-morning, and I am fighting to keep my hands off the phone in front of me. Less than twenty-four hours have passed since I made my commitments to Jackie, but already I know my willpower is broken. I need to call the coroner. Need to hear firsthand that the man with the bouncing body did, in fact, die of an overdose. I've got a plan all worked out, and when I can fight the urge no longer, I pick up the receiver and put my plan into action.

"Coroner's Office."

"Yeah, hi, this is Jeff Bell calling with KCBS Radio."

"KCBS? What can we do for you guys today?"

"Well, I'm looking to do a story about unresolved deaths in the area and was hoping to talk with someone from your staff."

The receptionist disappears to find a staff assistant to help me. Last chance, I think to myself. Still not too late to pull out here, save myself from committing this unthinkable breach of journalistic integrity. Hang up the phone. Hang up the—

"Ya-hello."

This is it, my whole career on the line. Can I really go through with this blatant lie? Really compromise everything I've worked for in nine years of broadcasting? Really sell myself out like a hooker trading her own dignity for some quick cash?

It's the only way, Doubt whispers back.

"Uh, yeah, hi, Jeff Bell here from KCBS."

The genie is out of the bottle, and there's no way to put her back in. What else can I do now but resort to my plan? With the cunning and finesse of a veteran con man, I launch into an elaborate story about tracking unexplained deaths for a possible series. I hate myself more with every word that spills out of my mouth.

"Didn't I run across a story in the wires just last week about some body found near a curb in your county?" I ask.

The assistant has to think for a minute. "Yeah, that rings a bell," he says very matter-of-factly.

"You guys ever figure out the deal with him?"

"Nah, still no positive ID."

"How 'bout the cause of death?"

"Pretty clear OD, as I recall."

Bingo!

We talk for a few more minutes before I thank the unsuspecting assistant for his time and lie that I might be calling back for more information for my series.

"No problem," he says. "Glad to help any time."

As I hang up the phone, the reality of what I've just done hits me with the force of a speeding locomotive.

ten

▶▶FF

fast-forward 3 days

Fluoxetine. Sertraline. Fluvoxamine. Paroxetine. Citalopram. The names all sound so wicked to me, like labels for some hideous poison an exterminator might use on the most hardened of rodents. They are, in fact, the clinical names of six antiobsessional medications known as selective serotonin reuptake inhibitors, or SSRIs, and with great resistance, I am learning everything there is to know about each.

My research comes on the heels of a total meltdown in Jackie's office and in advance of my scheduled meeting with the psychopharmacologist in Berkeley to whom Jackie has referred me. I still can't believe that I'm going on medication, and I hate my-self for ever agreeing to do so, but not nearly so much as I hate myself for my call to the coroner, a moral transgression so nefarious that I can share it with no one, including Jackie. I just danced around the whole thing the next day as I sat in her office and watched my emotions unravel, one fragile strand after another. Then Jackie spelled it out for me. "I can't help you, Jeff, if you're unwilling—or unable—to do the hard work that's needed." And that's when we got back on the topic of meds and how they might fit into my recovery program. After three or four adamant no's, a muffled yes somehow slipped out of my mouth.

So now here I am doing more investigative re-porting, ferreting out every tidbit on SSRIs that I can from my stack of OCD books. Like most of the hard facts about this mysterious disease, these are about as hard as soggy corn flakes. The experts agree, for example, that SSRIs work to block the reabsorption of a neurotransmitter called serotonin at the syn-apses between nerve cells, thereby increasing its availability in key areas. But precisely *why* this is beneficial, no one's entirely sure.

Not exactly the most reassuring of explanations.

Jackie has promised that I'll need to stay on meds only as long as it takes me to master her behavior-therapy skills. While that time frame re-mains to be seen, at least one of my books suggests that nearly half of all OCs on medication need to maintain at least a low dosage of their drugs for a good many years to avoid major relapses. This, more than anything, has me questioning everything. I just can't handle the notion that I might forever be dependent on some little pill to keep me alive.

Apparently, I'm not the first OC to struggle with this concept; it seems enough before me have to warrant a whole section on the topic in one of my books. I should compare my illness with diabetes, I'm advised in *Getting Control*. A diabetic needs insulin to live a normal life, the argument goes, so what's so bad about an OC needing anti-compulsive medication to function normally? *But medical problems are different*, I shout at the book, only to read on to the reminder that OCD is a chemical disorder.

Yeah. Maybe. But it's still different, I know, and no book could ever convince me otherwise.

II PAUSE I'm guessing you've already picked up on this fact, but still, it's probably worth noting here that an obsessive-compulsive's world is black and white. One hundred percent so. Shades of gray just don't exit, perhaps because our brains are incapable of processing them. Things are either good or bad, right or wrong, acceptable or unacceptable. All things. Always.

I've lost track of how many "normal people"

have told me they just can't understand my early aversion to meds. *(You recognized you were sick, you wanted to get better, you knew the pills could help.)* But that's because they're normal. I'm certain other OCs would understand the logic I applied in those days: People are either crazy or sane. People who take psychopharmacological drugs are crazy. Take the pills, and I concede I'm crazy. *Quod erat demonstrandum,* or Q.E.D., as my geometry teacher used to say.

No doubt it was this same black-and-white framework that made telling my closest relatives about my new label one of the most difficult things I'd ever done. How *does* one go about telling family that the son or brother or in-law they seem to know so well is not at all the person they think he is? That he's been diagnosed with a chronic brain disorder and is, in fact, by definition, mentally ill? Damned if I knew how. Phone calls? A press conference? Singing telegrams?

In retrospect, any of the above probably would have made more sense than the approach I ultimately opted for: a long, rambling letter that began, "It's time for me to do some explaining" and ended, "Pretty heavy stuff, all this information I just laid on you . . . I really don't know how comfortable I'm going to be talking about this for a while." On the many pages in between, I wrote out what I could about my recent research and Jackie and the meds I was about to go on. I also inserted a photocopy of the driving anecdote from *The Boy Who Couldn't Stop Washing,* explaining how a similar episode—and not a work delay—was the real reason I'd been hours late arriving to a recent family party. And I did my best to connect a long series of other dots for them.

Talk about a bombshell! No one knew what to say, or even whether to say anything, given my own request not to broach the subject just yet.

In the weeks and months that followed, there were comments here and there, but mostly awkward smiles, the kind we all resort to when words aren't really an option. Mandi sent me what struck me then, as it strikes me now, as the perfect care package—a big bag of Hershey's Hugs—and Mom, bless her heart, called several times to tell me (1) how much she loved me, and (2) that my father was reading everything he could on the subject. "You know, it's his way of dealing with things like this," she explained.

As for me, I spent countless nights imagining the damage my incriminating note could do to my permanent record and contemplating whether I should ask for all the copies back. If someone had told me that a decade later I'd share the stuff of that note with anyone caring to read it, I'd have deemed that person even crazier than I considered myself.

PLAY Samantha comes with me to Berkeley for my first meeting with the pharmacologist (whom I'll call Dr. Smith). We wander Shattuck Avenue on our way to his office, and the irony hits me. Here we are in one of the craziest cities in America, passing old beatniks and hippies left over from past decades on one street corner, long-haired preachers barking doomsday prophecies on another. Yet even they, and the rest of their fellow societal misfits, are capable of carrying out the many basic functions that are quickly slipping out of my reach, like driving a car and spending time around kids. And how about all these addicts taking refuge in the narrow doorways around us? They too, I decide, have a leg up on me. At least they're not on drugs because some doctor told them they *really should* be.

At ten o'clock, we knock on a door marked Dr. Smith. Two minutes later, Sam and I stuff ourselves into the cramped quarters that serve as his office. Lots of books on his shelves; lots of degrees on his walls; and behind his desk, a man in a button-down Oxford with wire-rimmed glasses and a neatly trimmed beard. Definitely not your typical Berkeley resident.

"Jackie says the meds will only be temporary," I volunteer seconds after our brief introductions.

Dr. Smith stares back at me, expressionless, and I try my best to read his reaction.

Nothing.

110

"You see, it all started two years ago with this boat mishap that—Well, no, actually, it really started when I was just a kid, with all these thoughts that would get stuck in my head—"

Still nothing from the doctor. I'm missing something here. I let my confusion show on my face.

"Dr. Persons has briefed me on your history," he finally says.

My *history*? What the hell is that: a loony's permanent-record equivalent of a criminal's rap sheet? Does it sit in some shrouded filing cabinet that all members of the Clandestine Psychiatric Society of America have access to once they master the secret handshake? I'm getting a good case of the creeps.

"Dr. Persons and I do a lot of work together," he continues. "We've had a great deal of success combining cognitive behavioral therapy with short-term drug treatment."

Now I get it, and I feel like an idiot. I'm not here to reinvent the wheel, to tell my whole drawn-out story to yet another shrink. Dr. Smith is Jackie's drug expert. He's going to implement and supervise whatever medication plan the two of them have devised. Psychologists don't dispense pills. Psychopharmacologists do. It's a tag-team sort of thing.

I shut up and let Dr. Smith launch into an overview of the various options for my drug treatment program. After my hours of research, I'm with him every step of the way.

"I think we should start with fluoxetine and see how you respond," he decides.

"That's Prozac," I say. "Isn't it used to treat depression?"

"Yes, but in lower doses than we typically need to tackle OCD."

Great. Now we've established where I stand on the Universal Nutcase Scale.

"I'm afraid of drugs," I say.

"A lot of people are. We'll help you through that."

"But I don't trust my senses as is. How can I be sure the meds won't make me even less responsible?"

"You're going to have to trust us."

"There *are* side effects though, right?"

"Yes, there are," Dr. Smith says, handing me a slip of paper, the AMA's *Fluoxetine/Sertraline Patient Medication Instruction Sheet.* "You should also know that many OCs need a good four to six weeks before they experience any real antiobsessive benefits from the medication."

We talk for a few more minutes and arrange to meet again in about three weeks. Dr. Smith encourages me to call if I have any questions.

■

The drug effects kick in for me in a matter of days, not weeks, and the first thing I notice is how jittery I feel. It's almost like that overly keen sense of perception six cups of coffee gave me after an all-nighter in college. Even the slightest sounds and movements grab my attention and make me jump—yet somehow only within the confines of my skin. I keep looking down expecting to see my whole body shaking, only to find that I'm standing still as can be.

As much as I'd like to deny it, I know the pills are also having a positive impact on my neurotransmission system, at least when it comes to my *what-if?* thoughts. The disturbing recurring questions still pop into my head, and frequently, but it's almost as if they now have to compete for attention with a whole slew of normal thoughts about everyday things—*Hey, I wonder what's for dinner; that's a great outfit on Sam; Brianna sure is growing up quickly*—those sorts of mundane observations I never even realized were missing.

The most pronounced effects of my medication, though, are not medical ones. They are the emotional by-products of my struggle to come to terms with this whole drug-taking concept. I've read Dr. Smith's list of possible side effects again and again, and while I've experienced none of them, a few of the "precautions" still scare the hell out of me. One in particular is especially disturbing: "If you are taking fluoxetine, dizziness, lightheadedness, or fainting may occur . . ."

Dizziness? Lightheadedness? Fainting? And I'm

supposed to trust myself to get behind the wheel of a car or walk through crowded places? I don't think so! The possibilities are endless for the new damage I could inflict. How ironic that these wonder pills that are supposed to be making me all better are, at the same time, giving my monster, Doubt, so much new ammunition.

eleven

fast-forward 3 months

We are making progress, Jackie and I. Week after week, she tightens the limits on my compulsive rituals, and week after week, I learn I can survive with that much less checking and rechecking of everything around me. We pore over charts of my time spent ritualizing and plots of the intensity levels of my various obsessions. There's no question things are moving in the right direction. "But it's time to notch up your discomfort level," Jackie tells me one morning in late December, four months after our first session together. "I want you to start tackling some serious exposure/response-prevention exercises."

I stare at her and shake my head. "You're kidding, right?"

"No. And don't look surprised. We talked about this. You need to start *exposing* yourself to more of your fears."

"Why? They seem to find me just fine on their own."

"But that's the point," Jackie says. "You'll only be ready to deal with them when they hit if you've conditioned yourself first."

"And I do that by . . . ?" I know the answer.

"Learning to sit with the fear. If driving down narrow streets still gives you the creeps, then we need to send you down five of them a day and keep you from looping back for a look at the damage. Do this enough and you'll desensitize to the fear. Trust me."

Trust is not the issue here. I am exhausted—physically, mentally, emotionally—in ways I didn't even know were possible. I'm in no mood to pick fights with Doubt. I tell Jackie that her timing stinks, that I'm just starting to feel as if life is getting back to normal.

"Normal, huh? You really think so?"

"Yeah," I say, but I see the trap I'm walking into. I know she thinks I'm in denial about the extent of my challenges.

"Okay, then let's take a little inventory, shall we."

Jackie is all smiles now as she scribbles a note on my weekly homework sheet. She always takes such pleasure in calling my bluffs.

"Here's the deal," she says. "I want you to keep a log of every OCD episode you battle over the next seven days."

"That's it?" I smart off, knowing it's not.

"Almost. I also want you to go over your list when you're done, then try to make sense of it relative to everything we've been talking about."

II PAUSE Over the course of our work together, Jackie sent me home with dozens of assignments—far too many of which I blew off entirely without ever confessing as much to her. This particular logging exercise, however, was one I gave my full attention to. And today, with the benefit of hindsight, I can see how significant it proved to be, largely because of what it made me face: the reality of just how much of my life Doubt had stolen from me.

I'll spare you the tedious details of my journal entries for that week (you're welcome), but I can't help thinking that a quick overview here might prove as helpful to you as Jackie's exercise was for me—at least in understanding the complexity of my day-to-day life in the mid-1990s. Really, it all boiled down to six sets of time-gobbling compulsions, each one leading back to a single all-too-familiar obsession.

The Obsession. I can't speak for all obsessive-compulsives, but among my own circle of OC friends, we each have a root obsession—the heart of every other obsession we might ever have, and the driving force behind all our rituals. I sometimes think of it as the calculated work of our internal bully, the single most effective weapon our nemesis, Doubt, can conjure up to taunt us with. For me that root obsession has always been this: *What if, through my negligence, I unknowingly harmed, or might harm, someone or something?* The boat incident, the road cone episode, the Hawaii hubcap, the disappearing homeless guy—all fit this boilerplate to a tee, wouldn't you agree?

Most obsessions are triggered by particular events, and my notes from Jackie's logging exercise are filled with those: lane changes, spilled liquids, mysterious sounds, and so on. But as I also noted that week, some taunting thoughts are really more like "envelope obsessions."

I can't remember now if that's a Jackie term or one I've coined along the way. In either case, I've come to use it to describe those rotating intrusive thoughts that seem to lurk at the outer envelope of my consciousness. They're always right there, quietly waiting for a lull in the chaos of daily triggers, ready to strike at a moment's notice. The end of the day, first thing in the morning, the middle of the night: all are prime times for their attacks, as are vacations and traditionally "happy" occasions of any kind. When they hit, they hit hard—no matter how many times they've hit before—and they always lodge themselves front and center until a new, more pressing thought is ready to take over. This could be minutes, hours, or even days.

By the time of this logging exercise, most of the episodes you've read about had slipped into such an envelope mode, each demanding far less of my attention than it initially did, but each still packing every bit of its original punch.

Mental Checking. I know that by now you've got the gist of this one. The virtual tape reviews. The constant mental re-creations of one event after another, always in some futile attempt to un-stick some stuck thought about harm. Play. Rewind. Play. Rewind. You get it. But there's one other layer to this compulsion you should also know about. I call it "life reviewing," and it stems from Doubt's most unsolvable question: *What if you're just a horrible person?* Only one way to be sure, it tells me, and that's to look back on my life and rule out the possibility that I am, in fact, truly despicable.

Conveniently enough, this introduces a lifetime's worth of tapes, and back in the mid-1990s, I spent countless hours going through them, attempting to ferret out the evidence tapes—like the Potato Bug sequence that haunted me many a night. I am five years old in this tape, playing by myself in my parents' backyard planter box. I am pulling a potato bug apart into two even sections, as I learned to do from a group of kids on the kindergarten playground just hours before. With the fascination of a scientist, I am observing the phenomenon that the other kids had noted: that the two separated halves continue to move about independently.

Then at once there's a woman's voice. A familiar voice. It is my mother's.

"What on earth are you doing? How would you like it if someone did that to you?"

The tape ends here. But another one picks things up many hours later in the middle of the night. In this one, I am hiding beneath my covers, fighting off a persistent image of some elephant-like creature tearing my body in two. Mom's sweet voice is providing a soundtrack, with her words looping like a toy train on the smallest of tracks: *How would you like it if someone did that to you? How would you like it if someone did that to you? How would you like it . . .?* I am at the same time ashamed and terrified.

The two tapes offer few details beyond these, but reviewing them as an adult, I always needed more. I wanted to back up the first tape to the schoolyard scene and verify that someone else was leading this cruel and unusual experiment. Was I really only following their lead, or was mine the twisted mind that invented the idea?

I would replay the sequences again and again until, out of frustration, I'd switch to another time in my life and yet another tape I couldn't stop myself from reviewing.

Physical Checking. This is both the most common compulsion of an OCD checker, and the one that my normal friends tell me they can most relate to. "*I've* doubled back to my car to check the parking brake," one of them will say.

"Yeah, but have you ever walked back for a second look? Or a third, fourth, or fifth?" I'll ask them.

And that's when the inevitable raised eyebrows confirm for me the difference between people like them and people like me.

As is typical with OCD, a good many of my checking drills quickly morphed into checking *rituals*—that is, especially repetitive and predictable compulsions. By the time of Jackie's exercise, I had compiled quite a long list of these: inspecting my car from bumper to bumper after every trip; returning to the location of nearly every pothole I hit;

diagramming on paper every problematic lane change, turn, or other driving challenge; checking and rechecking every door and appliance at home before leaving for a weekend; and combing the papers for crimes and accidents I might be responsible for. (Pretty ironic for a guy in the news biz, eh?)

Reassurance Seeking. "But are you sure . . .?" Good God, did I use those four words ad nauseam! But are you sure we locked the front door? But are you sure that was just a pothole? But are you sure I had nothing to do with the sirens?

The questions were usually directed at Samantha, often over the phone in one of so many embarrassing calls from work. "I've already told you I think it's fine," she'd tell me, trying to walk that fine line between helping me cope, and counter-productively enabling my checking. "Yeah, but are you *sure*?" I'd plead. One assurance was never enough. I can think of no checking compulsion more shame-producing for me, or more tiring and challenging for Samantha. Jackie would later guide us both in bringing this under control.

Confessing. I'm sure Freud and his colleagues could offer plenty of explanations as to why OCs like me always feel so compelled to confess; all I know is that, at the time of this logging exercise, I could seldom stop myself. My confessing was a compulsion in every sense of the term, and it mattered not how inconsequential my "wrongdoing" might have been, or how convinced I might have grown that the other party really wouldn't care. Confessions always offered me quick, if only temporary, relief, since they robbed Doubt of an opportunity to suggest I would need to come clean. Take the dripping umbrella incident I noted on my log during this week: I'd been in a supermarket checkout line when I'd happened to notice two or three dime-sized drops of water by my feet. This was my fault, and people could slip and die if I didn't tell someone, so I apologized to the checkout clerk, who thanked me for telling him and called for a "Code seven in aisle three." Things got pretty embarrassing, as I recall, when the cleanup guy couldn't even find my "puddle."

Fixing/Reporting. Close cousins of confessing, these two particular compulsions have always been the domain of my alter ego, Captain Hazard, doing his all to save the world from itself. A real crowd-pleaser for those lucky enough to see this superhero in action.

In the early days, I was only responsible for those hazards I'd actually created, like the supermarket umbrella puddle, or the dangerous "chocolate mine" I'd set that same week, when I dropped a piece of my Reese's Peanut Butter Cup while walking through downtown San Francisco. (I kid you not: I spent five minutes hunched over in pouring rain, combing a busy street corner, determined to find the remnants so no one could be hurt by them. Just *how*, even I can't begin to fathom.) But somewhere along the way, Captain Hazard expanded his scope to include any possible trouble spot with which he'd had contact. From then on, if I'd step on a single shard from a broken bottle, I'd need to get a broom and clean up every other piece up and down the street. Glass is usually easy enough to avoid, but twigs and rocks are also potential hazards—a bike tire could always hit one and lose its traction—and this meant dealing with just about everything I'd step on, short of the concrete itself. Sadly, walking soon presented almost as many challenges as getting behind the wheel of a car.

My direct-contact criterion also lead to my responsibility for every wobbly or broken chair I sat in—and man, did I have a knack for finding the one chair in a theater with half its hinge missing. Restaurant managers and theater ushers heard from me frequently.

And then, when I got too damn good at avoiding contact with even the smallest of hazards, I managed to begin obsessing about those I just happened to spot. I mean, *who was I to pretend I didn't see that nail lying there?* So now I'd have to fix these potential dangers too—or at least report them to someone.

No rest for Captain Hazard.

Avoiding. Technically, I suppose, this is not so much a compulsion as a consistent by-product of many of them. An OC grows to hate his obsessive-compulsive cycles so much that he'll do anything to steer clear of them. So while a trip to a McDonald's Playland might have made my daughters, and therefore me, very happy in those days, it usually wasn't worth the price I'd have to pay if I had to get near other kids I might harm. Stay away and I could avoid the inevitable *What if I hurt the kids?* thoughts and the various mental and physical checking drills that would surely follow. Unfortunately, avoidance is what psychologists call a *negative reinforcement.* Flee at the peak of fear, and you can't help but reinforce its power.

Good avoidance, I learned, takes a great deal of planning. Certain bad things are bound to happen in the future. Things like homeless people's deaths, unexplained accidents, and mysterious fires. Ironically, in my chosen profession, I hear about, and often report on, a great many routine tragedies. The odds are pretty good that a fair number of them will fall within the geographic and time "proximities"—many blocks and several hours, respectively—of my various car trips, thereby making me a possible suspect.

But wait, there's more. Like potential hazard issues, these issues managed to grow in breadth and scope, and it wasn't long before they extended far beyond driving. Soon structure fires on a block I'd

walked down could become the result of my negli-
gence (perhaps I'd kicked a gas main by accident).
Heart attacks within a building I'd visited might
later prove to be the result of something I'd said or
done. No situation was outside my ability to have
brought about harm, and reasonable association was
all the proof I'd need. Bottom line: it was always best
to protect myself from future trouble by avoiding the
homeless and high-crime areas, and by checking on
any situations that could become news down the
road. Best possible approach: leave the house as seldom as possible.

Looking back, it's hard to say just how much of all
this I managed to put together for myself during the
seven days of my logging assignment. I do know that
the whole thing had the sobering impact of a hot
shower gone cold, and that it would prove the perfect precursor for the exercise Jackie had waiting for
me next.

twelve

fast-forward 2 weeks

There's a sound BART trains make as they wend their way through the myriad curved tunnels that comprise the Bay Area Rapid Transit grid. It's a shrill, high-pitched screech. Metal rasping and straining against metal as unyielding steel rails and the wheels of one train car after another engage in a ferocious battle with the centrifugal forces of nature. For years I never even noticed the sound, but now, in early 1995, it's all I can hear every ride—the whistling, the whining, the visceral protest that cries out to the world. I know this ugly wail. It's the same one that bellows in silence from some tortured place deep inside of me.

It's mid-January now, and I am all but living on BART trains. I take them to my writing shifts at Channel 2. I take them to my air shifts at KCBS. And I take them to my weekly visits with Jackie. I have, for all practical purposes, given up driving, though I tell myself this is only temporary, that I'm only doing it to concentrate on the many non-driving OCD challenges I still need to tackle. This is a ludicrous argument, I know, and I don't dare share it with Jackie, who continues to assign me exposure exercises that I write down every week and then do nothing about.

Giving up driving has presented a whole slew of new challenges, not the least of which is my ability to cover street reporting shifts when asked by KCBS. Unbeknownst to my bosses, I've begun ditching our official news vehicles blocks from the station and hailing taxis to get out to my assignments. Hard to make money when I'm paying a cabbie to shuttle me around town, but at least it allows me to hang onto my job.

The harshest of all the consequences of my self-imposed license suspension, however, is the contribution it's making to my growing depression. If going on meds was a concession to my mental illness, then giving up driving is an all-out surrender.

I am, it would seem, no longer part of mainstream society. No longer capable of assuring my own survival.

I think about all of this, and the familiar cry of the BART trains too, as I sit in Jackie's cramped waiting room, working my way through the so-called "Beck Inventory" she has me fill out every week. In front of me on a clipboard are twenty-one sets of scored personal statements, and I'm supposed to choose the ones that best describe my feelings over the previous week. It's that damn second set that skews my score upward every time:

> 0 points: I am not particularly discouraged about the future
>
> 1 point: I feel discouraged about the future
>
> 2 points: I feel I have nothing to look forward to
>
> 3 points: I feel the future is hopeless and things can't improve

Week after week, another two or three points conceded.

I used to tally my Becks just for kicks. But then one day I asked Jackie about the scale and learned that my scores routinely exceed the standard threshold for clinical depression. So now I figure, why add to my funk by confirming its existence?

Jackie ushers me in to her office at 10:35, and I notice right away that something is different from our usual setup. It's a tape recorder—a cheap Radio Shack model—perched on the small table between our two chairs. It takes me a minute to remember why it's there, but when I do, all kinds of permanent-record issues start putting me on edge.

"We'd talked about recording an 'imaginal exposure' today," Jackie says, her eyebrows lifted just enough to invite a response.

"No, I don't think so," I tell her dismissively.

"How 'bout if I promise to give you the tape when we're done? No one, including me, will ever get to hear it." Jackie seems to understand my security paranoia.

"Then why bother making it?"

"Because I want *you* to listen to it—and often," she says. "Remember, our goal with this is to create a detailed mental picture of your very worst fear and then expose you to it over and over again until your distress level starts dropping."

My first thought is: this woman truly missed her calling as a torture expert for some interrogation squad with the special forces. My second is: could this really be any worse than my own virtual tape reviews? I'm skeptical that an "imagery" drill could have any value, but I've come to trust Jackie, and after a second confirmation that the tape will go home with me, I agree to play one round of her game.

Jackie smiles and gives me an approving nod, then reaches down and hits the Record button.

"So . . . what is it that's stressing you out these days?"

"Believe it or not, the Bouncing Body is back," I tell her, explaining that a recent hit-and-run story I covered has helped elevate this episode from its more dormant *envelope* status.

"Good," Jackie says. "Walk me through all your worst fears from this one."

"That's a short walk," I throw back at her. "The homeless guy is dead because I hit him."

"Is it really that simple?"

"Yeah. I kill the guy. It ruins the rest of my life."

"Right. Okay, so the police come and get you and—"

"Well, no," I interrupt. "The police don't know it's me."

"But that's good, right? Then you won't have to spend the rest of your life behind bars." Jackie is toying with me. She wants me to spell everything out.

"Come on. You know it's not 'doing time' that I find so fearful."

"Okay. Then just what is it?"

"Not *knowing* whether or not I killed the guy!"

I've got to believe my exasperation with Jackie is coming through loud and clear on the tape rolling between us.

"So you're okay with the idea that you killed this guy, as long as the cops know it was you?"

"Well, it's not like I'm saying that would be a great scenario—"

"But it's a better one than the possibility that the guy is fine but you'll never know that?"

"Right. No! I mean—"

"Well, isn't that noble, Jeff! I thought you said your worst fear was that you killed this poor homeless guy."

Jackie is in her element now, showing off her prosecutorial skills, taking me all this way so I'll make the confession she knows will come next.

"Okay, I get it. My worst fear is *not* that I killed some guy. It's that I'll never know for sure what happened to him."

"Good. Good!" Jackie is genuinely pleased with me, pleased with herself too, I'm guessing. "*Now* we can really get started. I want you to describe for me everything that happens because of all your uncertainty over this guy's fate."

I start with the obvious: a detailed rundown of each and every one of the compulsive effects of my doubts running wild.

Ten minutes into my litany, Jackie interrupts me.

"Consequences, Jeff. We need to get all the consequences of those compulsions down on this tape."

"Consequences?"

"Right. What's the bottom line here?"

I take a few moments to consider the question.

"Okay. I spend so much time reviewing the whole thing in my head that I can't focus at all at KCBS or Channel 2."

"Good. So what happens—do you lose your jobs?"

"Yeah. I lose my jobs and my whole career."

"And Samantha has to work full time now to support the family?"

"Right. But she can't leave the kids home with me, 'cause I'm spending all my time going back to that fateful intersection to check things out."

"Does Sam leave you, Jeff? Is that what happens next?"

I think about the question for a second or two. "No. She'd never do that. I'm the one—the one who . . ."

"The one who . . .?"

I need another second here to shiver away the prospect of losing my wife and daughters.

Okay. I'm all right. I can do this.

"I'm the one who moves out . . . to save the family."

Jackie sees my face getting wet. She hands me the box of Kleenex that's near the tape recorder.

"What's next," she whispers. "Where does it go from here?"

I know the answer. But I can't get it out of my mouth. I'm shaking too much from the crying.

"Nuhhhh. Nuhhh. Nuhhht house. I'm in a nut-house."

"Good, Jeff." Jackie's voice is barely audible. I can't see her because my eyes are closed. "Keep going with it, Jeff."

"The images," I babble. "I can't stop myself from playing them back even here. I can't stop . . ."

The sound of my own wailing is unbearable now. I force myself to stop crying, but it takes all the squeezing pressure I can apply with my eyelids.

And then there is silence. Dead air, as we say in radio, for at least thirty seconds.

Finally, a loud click. I realize Jackie has stopped the tape.

"Congratulations, Jeff. I think you got us precisely where we needed to go."

thirteen

PAUSE

Okay, so here's where telling this story gets tricky for me. Sharing my virtual tapes with you is easy; as I've said, they play and replay in my head to this day. But for all the extensive image sequences I have access to, there are also gaps, and one of these, I'm now convinced, is more significant than anything in my archives. It's kind of like Nixon's missing Watergate tapes, I suppose, except instead of having Rosemary Woods or anyone else to blame, I can only point the finger at fatigue or something bigger than me that I wasn't meant to understand.

The gap at issue here doesn't belong to my 1995

tapes, but rather to one recorded fourteen years earlier that will forever be linked to them. I am sitting at my bedroom desk in this well-worn tape, a seventeen-year-old kid with a pencil and paper in hand and no idea what to do with either of them. It's late at night, a week or two before my high school graduation, and I am struggling to write the valedictory address I'm expected to give—a speech that was supposed to be my shining moment of glory after four years of busting my hump to get into the U.S. Naval Academy. Just weeks before, Congressman Tom Lantos had made that lifelong dream a reality with his official "appointment." But then came the physical. And the series of failed color identification tests. And the call from my recruiter saying how sorry he was to inform me that the U.S. Navy has no need for colorblind sailors.

So now on this night back in '81, I am wishing like hell that I didn't have to get up in front of my classmates. I am still reeling from the biggest blow that life has ever dealt me. Still feeling sorry for myself, incapable of understanding that my failed physical will later save me from years worth of uniformed embarrassment dealing with a handicap much greater than colorblindness.

The theme of our graduation is "This Is It," a message borrowed from one of the year's biggest pop hits. I'm supposed to somehow incorporate this theme in my speech, and my first attempts have failed miserably. And still I have no ideas, only a blank piece of paper and a pencil with teeth marks all around it. Soon it's nine o'clock. And then ten. And then eleven. I am starting to panic.

But then, poof, it's the middle of the night, and I am staring at a speech I can't remember writing:

> "There have been times in my life I've been wondering why. Still somehow I believed we'd always survive. . ." Songwriter and vocalist Kenny Loggins recently gave us those words of encouragement in his hit song "This Is It." I hope tonight to make his message my own.
>
> Belief: It's a true wonder to me that in just six letters so much could be expressed and implied. One word, so vague, and yet so significant in all of our lives. Belief, as I see it, can be broken down into three distinct concepts: Belief in ourselves; belief in others; and belief in life . . .

My sappy little speech—later preserved for eternity on my parents' IBM Selectric—went on to offer an elaborate trifurcated explanation of the workings of belief and its ability to help us do anything—*"Yes, anything"*—including overcome incredible challenges. After a handful of bad clichés and random thoughts on such matters as integrity and strength and faith and possibility, my sermon-like essay wrapped up with an admonishment to my classmates that now is the time to believe, because, well . . . *This Is It.*

I remember my confusion and the sense of wonder that came with it as I first read through my penciled scribbles that early morning back in '81. Not only was I at a loss to explain how the words had gotten there, I was also in awe of how much they instantly meant to me. *Belief in myself, in others, and in life—all working toward some greater good. Yeah, that's what it's all about, isn't it?* At seventeen, profound thinking is finding meaning in a Stones song, or getting more out of a movie than just a few laughs. Yet there I was that morning, with my whole life in front of me and no plans to speak of— save for the ones that had just been pulled out from under me—and what was I doing? Contemplating the meaning of life. Weird.

A few days after my grad speech experience, I decided what I really needed was to go discover America, and perhaps myself along the way. So I purchased a thirty-day Greyhound Ameripass, a backpack, a stack of books, and a cheap silver-plated dog tag onto which I paid a mall engraver to etch the word *Believer*. If I wasn't going to be a Naval officer as I'd always planned, I knew I needed a new image of myself to hold. I also knew that whatever else I might someday decide to be, I wanted first and foremost to be a guy who lived by that graduation speech.

The month that followed was unlike any before it. After years of battling to control my own destiny and everything around me, I somehow managed to let it all go. Reaching for my dog tag again and again, I toured cities by day and talked with fellow backpackers by night. Read Plato on the bus and wrote poetry in meadows. Laughed off a close call with would-be muggers in D.C. and drank moonshine with a sweet old man in the South. Never before had I felt so in tune with life and all its offerings. Never again, I now realize all these years later, would I ever feel so free.

I can't remember just when after the bus trip I stopped wearing the dog tag. What I do know is when and why I put it back on: it was shortly after my brief nuthouse visit with Jackie, and it was because of the identity meltdown I found myself battling in the early weeks of '95. Doubt, I was learning, consumes from the inside out, and with each passing day, it gnawed away that much more of my core. The guy in the mirror still looked about the same, but no longer could I recognize much beyond his reflection.

Night after night, the nagging questions haunted me: Whatever happened to that carefree kid on the Greyhound? What would he, the great aspiring believer, think of me, the pathological doubter? How devastated would he feel, watching me try to walk away from my parked car, checking and rechecking the doors and parking brake, incapable of believing even my own physical senses? Our only common link, it would strike me in moments of bone-chilling reality, was this weathered dog tag I'd catch myself sliding back and forth on its chain, begging it to remind me of what I once fancied myself to be, and how to get there again.

I can't help thinking today that, somehow, some way, my pleading must have worked.

▶ On a brisk morning in February I shake off
PLAY the cold, along with my skepticism, and enter a rustic office building marked "Center for Attitudinal Healing."

A receptionist looks up from her desk and asks if she can help me find anyone or anything in particular.

"Just looking for some background information," I tell her, imagining for a second how lost I must seem.

"Are you interested in taking part in one of our support groups, or in volunteering?" she asks.

"Actually, neither at this point," I say, knowing I've come here today for an entirely different reason.

I am here, truth be told, to see for myself that

this place and the man who founded it back in 1975 are real. I have spent days reading about Dr. Gerald Jampolsky, his original vision of providing support for children battling cancer and other terminal illnesses, and the subsequent expansion of his practice to people of all ages facing a variety of life crises. I know that his "power to choose" counseling approach, based loosely on the teachings of *A Course in Miracles*, has proven so successful that nearly a hundred independent centers in more than a dozen countries have taken root from it.

I also know that Dr. Jampolsky's remarkable accomplishments have drawn the attention of media programs from *60 Minutes* to *Phil Donahue* and the *Today* show, and that his Center Advisory Board has attracted such luminaries as Dr. Linus Pauling, Fred Rogers, Archbishop Desmond Tutu, and singer John Denver. But as always, I am skeptical, and I need to see with my own eyes that this work exists.

Not since *The Boy Who Couldn't Stop Washing* has any book given me as much hope as Jampolsky's *Change Your Mind, Change Your Life*—this despite the fact that it has nothing to do with overcoming OCD, per se. The book simply affirms the human spirit's power to triumph over incredible physical and emotional challenges. At its root is this basic premise: that our thoughts and attitudes determine how we see the world, and that we ourselves choose those very thoughts and attitudes.

Freedom of choice is not something I'm exercising much of these days. Doubt feeds me one horrific *what-if* thought after another. And I, without question, give these thoughts all my attention. Time after time after time. But what if I didn't have to? What if I could willfully choose to do otherwise?

Jampolsky says I can—much as any of the young cancer patients he works with can choose to see beyond the nagging, fearful thoughts of their futures. No, they can't choose to be rid of their disease, but they *can* decide not to focus their attention on their sick bodies and their fears about death. Instead, they can choose to see their shared predicament as an opportunity to give of themselves for a greater good—to help others with cancer, for example. Through support groups, pen-pal networks, writing projects, and the like, these brave young souls are willfully shifting their attention, and in so doing, finding peace and comfort in service to others.

It's all about the "movies" we choose to make and to watch, says Jampolsky, referring now to the big picture that even those of us without catastrophic illnesses must sort out for ourselves. (For obvious reasons, this particular analogy piques my interest.) Imagine that in your mind is everything necessary to make a movie, he suggests in *Love Is Letting Go of Fear*. What we experience in our daily lives then is simply our own state of mind projected onto a screen of the world. The thing is, Jampolsky warns, we each have two internal directors vying to control our movies: a love-based one that recognizes our inherent good in this very moment; and a fear- or ego-based one that thrives on keeping us from knowing who we really are, largely by miring us in the past and future. *We* choose which of these dueling directors is in charge—and thereby what we see of the world—simply by choosing which of the two we invest in with our own innate free will.

Just how all this relates to me and my particular challenges, I'm not entirely sure. What I do know though is that I invest *my* everything in fear and its twin called Doubt, and I sure as hell watch a lot of fear-and-doubt-based movies—literally, in my head, and figuratively, on the screen of the world, as Jampolsky puts it. My "ego director," it would seem, is this internal voice I've dubbed Doubt. As for the other director, I can't help thinking that perhaps this role belongs to whatever it was that the old dog tag–wearing *Believer* in me had once taken its cues from.

I'd love to run this whole theory by the receptionist, who is now handing me a schedule of upcoming Center events, but I wouldn't know where to start. Fortunately, our brief conversation, together with my quick look around this place, has provided me with all the evidence I need to feel comfortable that Jampolsky's work is not just some façade to sell books, that his principles are really being employed in a real-life setting. I leave here knowing that I'm safe to peek at the vast world behind the curtain at which Jampolsky stands.

fourteen

fast-forward 1 week

Situation: Ambiguous intersection.

Obsession: I may have caused an accident by not having handled the turn lane properly.

Compulsions: Go back to look at the intersection. Re-create the turn repeatedly in my head. Listen to traffic reports for word of trouble.

Jackie and I are working our way through one of her so-called "Thought Record" worksheets, as we've done a hundred times before with a hundred other episodes. But this time, Jackie suggests I attempt to indulge my new interest in spiritual arguments as we tackle the worksheet's all-important *Responses* section.

"I have to be honest, though," she apologizes. "I know nothing about spiritual reasoning."

"That's okay," I tell her. "Neither do I."

A couple of heathens, we give it a shot.

Responses to Ambiguous Intersection Obsessions:

Perhaps I still can't trust myself, but I've given this job to God. If he's not showing a clear sign, I'm going to trust him and move on.

I could go back to the intersection and check, but this doesn't serve my greater function.

God judges us on intentions, not actions, and my intention was good.

God doesn't want me to suffer, obsess, and worry. I can serve him best if I just move on.

I need to work on letting this go.

This is a test of my faith and trust. I can come out of this stronger.

This is new territory for Jackie and me. I sense that she's a bit uncomfortable with the whole notion of introducing spirituality into our traditional cognitive behavior therapy. But Jackie is the quintessential pragmatist. If something seems to be working for one of her patients, then she'll do everything possible to encourage its continued use. For whatever reasons, spiritual reasoning seems to help me get some perspective on the whole intersection incident and a handful of other episodes in the weeks that follow. So we go with it, dancing around the many differences one might point to between a spiritual and a scientific approach to treatment, focusing instead on the surprising number of similarities.

II PAUSE As I'm sure you can appreciate, the real-world laboratory in which Jackie and I worked was anything but a controlled environment. So to say that my new commitment to spiritual principles quickly made a huge difference in my OCD battles would be to connect dots no good scientist would ever venture to link. My inner believer would love to claim the credit. But for all I know, my quantum-leap progress could have been due to my meds, which Dr. Smith had recently changed from Prozac to Zoloft. Or a sudden breakthrough in my understanding and application of behavior therapy. Or some harmonic convergence or planetary alignment. Who really knows? All I can tell you for sure is that I was soon able to cut in half my time spent checking, and perhaps more importantly, that I also managed to reclaim at least some semblance of my once healthy sense of humor.

From day one, Jackie had coached me to look for the humor in my ludicrous OCD thinking and checking patterns, often taking the task upon herself when so moved. Laughter is powerful medicine, as the old saying goes, but it can also be a tough pill to swallow. Fortunately (or unfortunately, depending on my frame of mind), Sam shared Jackie's sense of humor. Sam, at Jackie's urging, had been relentless in trying to drive home the droll nature of my illness, resorting even to verse to help me hear myself talk:

> *I killed a man in Frisco,*
> *One in Oakland too.*
> *Dead bodies, they surround me.*
> *Oh, what am I to do?*
>
> *They jump off towering bridges,*
> *Litter highways too.*
> *Dead bodies, they surround me.*
> *Oh, what am I to do?*
>
> *I force cars off the roadways,*
> *Cause strokes all over too.*
> *Dead bodies, they surround me.*
> *Oh, what am I to do?*

I have a slight disorder;
It's known as O-C-D.
With Jackie there to help me,
No more bodies will I see.

Jackie couldn't have been more delighted when I brought in my wife's "charming" prose. "You sure were lucky to find a woman like Sam," she'd said, all smiles. From then on, the two of them would share more than a few good laughs at my expense—perhaps none more relished than the ones spawned by the Ben Gay episode.

As I recall, it had all begun when I got home from the library one night and realized that the heating ointment I'd put on my shoulder for a sore muscle had left a mark on my shirt. This was not good. *I bet it also got on the library's couch!* Within seconds Doubt had me convinced that others who sat on that couch might get the ointment on them, perhaps putting their health at risk. *What about pregnant women? Is the product safe for them?* I had to know. Had to read the warnings on the label.

The tube of Ben Gay I'd used was still at the gym, so I had to go out to the drugstore that night and peruse the shelves. No serious warnings, as I remember, but that didn't stop me from returning to the library, where I spent a good ten minutes sniffing the couch—yes, nose to the cushions, *sniffing the couch.* Imagine the notation on my sacred permanent record had some authority figure caught me in the act!

Unlike my wife and therapist, *I* was far from amused by my actions that night. It was only at this juncture, months later, that I began to see anything even remotely funny about the whole incident. But the point is I *did,* and that point was not lost on Jackie.

"You're really laughing now about the Ben Gay episode?"

"Yeah."

"You really understand now what all that nonsense was about?"

"Yeah."

"I guess we really are making progress."

▶ Another bookstore. More research. But this
PLAY time I am scouring not bookshelves, but bulletin boards, looking for some kind of human support system I can tap into. Mentors. Coaches. Maybe just a group of people who understand suffering. Ever since learning about the groundbreaking group work at Jampolsky's Center for Attitudinal Healing, I've become fascinated by the power of shared determination. But I am not facing a catastrophic illness, nor am I grieving for a lost one, so the Center is out.

I don't know *where* I'm supposed to be. There are OCD support groups out there. I've heard of a few. But who'd want to sit around in a room with a bunch of freaks like me?

Today, though, I have stumbled across word of a "New Thought" discussion group that meets on Tuesday nights not too far from our house. At first, I dismiss the idea outright, imagining what kind of namby-pamby, touchy-feely types would choose to be a part of something like this. But then I remind myself that I can get up and walk out at any time. Nobody needs to know who I am. I can be a fly on the wall. Besides, when it comes right down to it, what on earth have I got to lose?

The following Tuesday, I fight a rainstorm and two nasty driving episodes as I make my way to the meeting. Dripping wet and ten minutes late, I attempt to sneak in the door marked with the address I've scrawled on a notepad along with directions. But a surreptitious entry is not to be. One step through the doorway and I am staring right into an oversized living room. Right at some thirty men and woman seated in a circle of folding chairs. They too are staring at me, alerted to my arrival by a door hinge in desperate need of some WD-40.

A soft-spoken man with graying hair and kind, tired eyes is standing at the far end of the room. He motions me in.

"Please. Make yourself comfortable. My name is Dirk and I moderate this group. Right now, we're just doing some sharing about our challenges this past week."

Thirty pairs of eyes are locked on mine. I want—*need*—to make up an excuse, tell them I'm in the wrong place, and get the hell out of here. But I can't. For whatever reason, this is exactly where I'm supposed to be, and whatever "knowing" tells me this also suggests I plant my butt in one of these seats. Now.

Over the course of the next forty-five minutes, I learn how off-base I'd been about who would attend this meeting. Not a single namby-pamby, touchy-feely type in the room. As it turns out, Dirk is a recovering alcoholic, clean and sober for nearly two decades now, and he and at least half of the other people in the room are here as part of their AA or other Twelve Step work. In no particular seating order around me are old men, kids barely out of their teens, a gray-haired woman with granny glasses, a hulking biker with mean tattoos, and a cast of some two dozen other miscellaneous characters, all joined by two common bonds: a heartfelt desire to rebuild their lives and a humble recognition that they can't do it alone.

Something else strikes me early on, too: no one is pressuring anyone to say anything or volunteer any thoughts. Hands go up. Dirk calls on people. And they, in turn, offer real-life, school-of-hard-knocks comments on the various spiritual topics that pop up in discussion. The whole dynamic is far more comfortable than I could have imagined. If I weren't so worked up over my driving episodes and my soggy umbrella's current potential to cause all kinds of problems, I might even be able to relax.

After the meeting, Dirk catches me on my way out the door. I thank him for his hospitality and brace myself for the sales pitch I know is coming.

"I'm glad you showed up," he says. "Please know you're welcome any time."

And that, along with a firm handshake, is all he's interested in pitching me.

Week after week, I show up for Dirk's Tuesday night group and quietly take in all the inspiring stories: a longtime drunk talking about the morning he woke up in a gutter and realized it was time to put his hands together in prayer; a recovering addict describing his life-changing revelation in prison; a former CEO explaining what it's like to wind up with a cardboard box for your home.

I say very little, just soak it all in. But as the weeks march on, I come to realize that I'm the guy who keeps pulling pennies from the jar next to the deli cash register to round out his bill, but never sees a need to toss an occasional coin from his own change back in the bin. Here I am drawing inspiration from recovering drunks and addicts, all brave enough to talk about their lives in the gutter, but I'm too embarrassed to open my mouth about driving in circles?

So one night, forty minutes or so into our meeting, I just do it: stand up and tell the group I have something to share. I get about three quarters of the way through my little speech before I start to lose it and scurry out of the room. Standing on the front porch, I realize what an egregious mistake I've just made. I decide to forgo the rest of the meeting and head home, leaving this place behind me forever. But damn it, my jacket is still inside.

I peek my head in the door and see that the group is just breaking up. My jacket is waiting for me right where I've left it. So too, it seems, is all of the personal encouragement I've been craving.

One by one they come over to me, arms outstretched. Tattooed and needled-pocked forearms wrap around my shoulders. Eyes set in faces weathered and chiseled by years of rough living look right into mine. Voices strengthened by a power greater than their own whisper in my ears.

"We're proud of you, Jeff."

"You can get through this, big guy."

"Your Higher Power is there for you. Always."

These are the *true* believers comforting me. Ragged, battered, patched-up souls who have learned the hardest way possible how to tap into the power of their own belief. They are walking their talk one day at a time, carrying each other when the journey calls for it.

If I, too, am going to stumble my way along some kind of pseudo-spiritual path, I know these are the travel companions I want by my side.

fifteen

fast-forward 2 months

The first two familiar figures I spot are Marcia Clark and Christopher Darden. I think that's Robert Shapiro just to my left. It's hard to tell. They all look so different in person, so much smaller and more ordinary, unframed by a television screen.

We are standing elbow to elbow, the four of us and at least fifty others, in a narrow wood-paneled foyer. Attorneys, family members, selected representatives of the general public, and a handful of credentialed reporters like myself, all waiting to help make, record, or witness an afternoon's worth of judicial history in the room just beyond us.

It's June 13, 1995. The "trial of the century" is in recess, about to resume here on the ninth floor of the Criminal Courts Building at 210 West Temple Street in Los Angeles. At any minute now, a bailiff will arrive to swing open the doors marked "Department 103" and usher us into Judge Lance Ito's courtroom, where I'll take my designated seat. And there I'll sit until the following recess, at which point another CBS-affiliated reporter will take over from me. After months of watching the O.J. Simpson trial on TV like millions of other Americans glued to their sets, I'm about to do what they can only dream of: take in America's ultimate soap opera with my own two eyes.

No question about it. This is the most coveted trial assignment of an entire generation of reporters, and here I am with an afternoon pass. Just one more huge opportunity to come my way in recent months.

The courtroom doors spring open at 2:40 and we file in. The media coordinator has given me general directions where to sit, but the tiny room—which is about a quarter of the size it appears to be on TV— is devoid of any helpful signs such as "Reporters Sit Here" or "Keep Out of This Area." I hope to God I'm plopping down in the right place. *Is the media section really* this *close to the jury box?*

By the time I settle in and confirm that the people to my immediate right and left are indeed reporters, all the key players have taken their places. Marcia Clark and Christopher Darden sit at the prosecution table, joined by their colleague from the district attorney's office, Brian Kelberg. To their left and across the center aisle sit Dream Teamers Johnnie Cochran and Robert Shapiro, along with several other staffers I can't seem to place. And there, stuffed into a chair right alongside them at the crowded defense table, wearing an expensive suit and an almost vacant expression, is the most infamous man in America: Orenthal James Simpson. O.J. The football legend. The Hertz guy. The murder defendant.

Within a few minutes, a bailiff announces the arrival of the honorable Judge Lance Ito. We all stand and the jurors enter their box. I watch with fascination as the men and women who will decide this case take their seats directly in front of me. Theirs are the faces the rest of the world can't see, hidden from the courtroom cameras, off limits to the hovering photographers, sequestered from society by a team of court-appointed security guards. I can't help feeling both privileged and uncomfortable now, having "special knowledge" of their true identities.

L.A. County's chief medical examiner, Dr. Lakshmanan Sathyavagiswaran, is testifying today, and Judge Ito instructs Brian Kelberg to continue his direct examination. Soon we are all listening to a grisly discussion about the fatal stab wounds to Ron Goldman's chest and thigh.

Maybe it's all the cameras. Perhaps it's just seeing such a well-known cast of characters all in one place. But this whole scene feels like a movie set to me, with all the key players going through predetermined motions and reciting scripted lines. My own fear director, Doubt, is hungry for a piece of the action and wants so badly to cast me as a walk-on villain.

Conveniently, the opportunity presents itself within minutes when I look up at the bench and see Judge Ito staring at me. Well, maybe he's just looking across the courtroom in general. *But how can I be sure? Have I done something wrong?* I know Ito has a penchant for throwing people out of his courtroom, expelling spectators for everything from chewing gum to whispering. But with the exception of an occasional pen click, I can't think of any noise infractions of which I might be guilty.

I look away from Ito and cast my glance straight ahead. But doing so leaves me staring right at the jury box not more than fifteen feet away. I know the alternate juror pool is nearly depleted these days in the wake of several recent dismissals. I also know that jurors can be booted for even the slightest communications with reporters. I put the two together and imagine what could happen if, inadvertently, I were to make eye contact with a juror or two, who, in turn, might be dismissed for trying to communicate with me. Doubt whispers that I could wield my enormous power and single-handedly derail the biggest trial of our time!

I can't let this happen. Can't even risk it by allowing my eyes to get anywhere near the men and women of the jury. But with the bench and the jury box now both off limits, I'm not sure *where* I'm supposed to be looking. OCD has found its trap.

Dr. Lakshmanan is testifying about blood pressure now, and I can feel mine rising. I am growing lightheaded, dizzy, buckling under the weight of this whole trial resting squarely on my shoulders. I need to get out of here, away from all this potential to make a mess of everything. Mercifully, Judge Ito calls a recess at around 3:30, and fifty minutes after entering the courtroom, my time is up.

The writing is on the wall. Given my struggles in the Simpson courtroom and my increasing difficulties just getting to the site of a story, my reporting days are clearly numbered—despite all my recent progress with Jackie.

The reality of this notion, though, is unacceptable.

I can try harder, and I do. I force myself to walk

away from my car on the first attempt when parking for an assignment, or I get creative with taxis and BART trains to avoid the whole issue altogether. I make every effort to get myself to the very center of a breaking news scene, even if it means nudging past thick crowds and police tape. And I try to take the fire chief at his word when he tells me it's okay to roll my tires over his hoses at the scene of a brush fire. But I am paying a huge personal price for my efforts. And I am fighting a losing battle.

There is a fine line, I am learning, between "believing in" and "fooling" oneself, and while I'm still not sure where I'm supposed to draw that line for myself, I know street reporting is on the far side of it. I can't imagine that any of my new AA friends would pursue a career in bartending. But isn't that, in essence, what I'm trying to do?

It's all about limits, I am coming to understand. But the consequences of that conclusion are all too sobering. At KCBS, like at most all-news stations, there are only a handful of full-time anchors who spend their entire shifts in the control room. Those of us who rotate in on a *part*-time basis are expected to be available for street reporting, as necessary, to cover all bases. It's a simple matter of scheduling, really. Short of explaining my story to my bosses, I can't think of any way to excuse myself from the street, and it's not as if any full-time anchoring slots are going to open up anytime soon. So my choices, when it comes right down to it, are but two: (1) find a way to handle my field reporting assignments at KCBS, or (2) look for a full-time anchoring position with some other station.

"Only an idiot would ever leave KCBS," a friend in the business once said to me after learning I had landed a job there. An idiot *or* an obsessive-compulsive, I think to myself as I begin sending out airchecks and resumes to news directors everywhere.

Nobody's hiring.

This is the mid-1990s. The entire radio business is shrinking as the effects of deregulation begin to kick in in earnest. Month after month, one giant corporation gobbles up another, only to be gobbled up itself by an even bigger player. "Do more with less" is the directive given to station managers everywhere from corporate bosses in out-of-state skyscrapers.

The growing uncertainty surrounding my future begins taking its toll. With each passing day, I spend that much more time checking my tapes and everything around me, even as I reread my Jampolsky books. And tug on my dog tag. And beg myself to believe. My Beck Inventory scores rise like mercury in a thermometer on a hot summer day.

And then, at long last, the phone rings in early July. It's an old boss of mine who now heads up sales for KFBK Radio in Sacramento.

"Our afternoon drive cohost is leaving us for a gig in Seattle," he starts off.

"Yeah?" I say, wondering if he's taking this conversation where I hope that he is.

"Yeah. You interested in talking?"

If leaving KCBS is idiocy, than leaving the fourth largest radio market in the country for one ranked twenty-seventh is probably pure lunacy. But market ranking becomes almost irrelevant when you're talking about a broadcasting powerhouse like KFBK. The station is legendary in the industry, with fifty thousand watts of power and market share ratings unmatched by all but a very few news-talks in America. Rush Limbaugh worked there just before going national. So, too, did Morton Downey, Jr. The station's newsroom is one of the best around, holding its own against the bigger staffs in San Francisco and Los Angeles. An open drive-time host position is a plum opportunity, no matter how you look at it, and I know I'd be an idiot *not* to at least go talk to KFBK.

Ten weeks and three visits to Sacramento later, I sign a lucrative two-year contract to join KFBK as its afternoon anchor. For better or worse, I am about to put eighty-five miles between me and—in no particular order—KCBS, Channel 2, Jackie, The Boat, my new Twelve Step friends, my parents, my childhood stomping grounds, and nearly four years' worth of OCD episodes.

■

James Marshall struck gold outside Sacramento back in 1848. On a Sunday in late September 147 years later, I pull into town to try my own luck.

From my first glimpse of the region, I realize it's much more than I ever anticipated. More spacious. More developed. More inviting. More comfortable. Everything new and old all in one place. Trees. Rivers. Mountains. Riverboats. Gold Rush era forts. Shiny highrises. A basketball arena. The state capitol and the governor's mansion. All right there, just a ninety-minute drive from San Francisco.

As for KFBK, it is everything the industry trades have made it out to be. From its plush modern studio to its well-seasoned staff, the operation is every bit as impressive as anything I've seen in L.A. or San Francisco. And with a seventy-three-year heritage of serving the community, KFBK truly *owns* this market. Locals don't just listen to the station, they take a personal stake in it.

News anchors at KFBK are actually news *personalities*—a fact pointed out to me many times during my long interviewing process. Just what this distinction means becomes quite clear to me as I get to know my new colleagues in general, and my new on-air partner in particular.

Her name is Kitty O'Neal, and she is without a doubt the best known and most loved woman in Sacramento. Now in her fourteenth year with KFBK, Kitty has done a little bit of everything for the station, from serving as Rush's high-profile producer back in the mid-1980s, to co-anchoring afternoons in more recent years.

A petite redhead with sparkling green eyes and a million-dollar smile, Kitty has also parlayed her radio success into an impressive television career, moonlighting for several years as an entertainment reporter for the local CBS affiliate and appearing in numerous commercials. Her face has graced the cover of *Sacramento Magazine,* and her emceeing talents have been employed by just about every service organization in town. Kitty is a huge star around here. She is also an exceptionally gracious woman. We hit it off from our very first conversation. Our bosses knew what they were doing, pairing us up as a team.

As fate would have it, O.J. and I meet up again on the afternoon of my KFBK debut, this time hundreds of miles apart. *I* am stepping up to this station's microphone for the very first time just as *he* is getting word that his jury has reached its verdict. The news crosses the wires right away, and my first three hours of airtime are rife with anticipation of the most awaited judgment since the Lindbergh trial. Superstitious broadcasters would say this is a good omen, a kiss from the mighty news gods who control such things.

Kitty and I quickly fill up a week's worth of shows with O.J. verdict analysis and reaction, debriefing all the major pundits and working off one another as if we've been doing this for years. In the studio and at home, I slip into my new life with the ease of someone trying on a custom suit, hand-tailored for a perfect fit. Sam and the girls arrive in Sacramento, and professional movers take care of all the shipping, compliments of my new employer. A free move to go along with all the other extras coming my way: trade scrip for restaurants all over town, lucrative endorsement deals, courtside tickets to see a Kings game at Arco Arena. Considering all these perks, and the publicity photo shoots, and the *Sacramento Bee*'s flattering announcement of my arrival, I'm thinking a guy could get used to the VIP treatment that seems to come with this whole "news personality" thing.

Best of all though, I'm finished for good with my OCD.

This, at least, is what I tell myself over and over again in the weeks that follow. Big stars don't fight daily battles with mental illness. I *am* a big star now. Therefore I am no longer mentally ill. Perfect logic, as far as I'm concerned, though not quite the argument I share with Jackie when I explain that I'm planning to go off my meds. She and I have arranged to talk on the phone every other week. Between her support and that which I'm finding at the non-denominational Unity church the girls and I have started attending, I'm certain I'll be fine.

"Your call," Jackie tells me. "Just be sure to talk with Dr. Smith about how to phase out the medication."

"Right," I say, just before taking my bottle of Zoloft pills and burying it deep in the medicine cabinet for all eternity. I don't need these damn things anymore. Period. So after more than a year of doing like Alice and "feeding my head," I simply stop cold turkey one day.

Whoa!

Almost overnight, life becomes an emotional balance beam. One minute I'm dangerously close to falling off to the left; the next I'm flailing my arms to keep from tanking to the right. Everything around me is all out of whack as my serotonin levels adjust to a post-Zoloft world. If OCD really is a matter of biochemistry, then I can only imagine how mixed-up things must be in the mad scientist's laboratory be-tween my ears.

But I power through, because I'm not turning back. And because I don't need medication. And be-cause I'm finished for good with my OCD.

sixteen

fast-forward 18 months

A double life. There's really no other way to describe my first year and a half in Sacramento, and I've got two distinct sets of tape segments to prove it. In one set—the cassette airchecks—I am the *news personality* KFBK hired to cohost its afternoon program. I am confident, in control, on top of my game. Together with Kitty, I cover live breaking news stories with ease, interview celebrities and the nation's top newsmakers, broadcast from remote locations all around town, and share familiar stories about my wife and kids. I am a friendly, credible, normal guy who thousands of afternoon commuters check in with daily as they battle the backups on I-80 and Highway 50.

But then there's my second set of tape segments—the virtual ones—which unfortunately tell a far different story. The guy in these archives is nothing short of a closet basket case. He sneaks around picking up twigs and rocks from the sidewalk. And checking his parking brake and doorlocks again and again. And driving his car in endless circles.

And he spends ever more of his life hiding in bathrooms, scrubbing his hands.

This is my latest trick, and I can't remember just when it kicked in, though I do know it grew out of a story I covered about an outbreak of hepatitis C spawned by a single pair of unsanitary hands. *Perfect*, Doubt chided me. *You can't let that happen, now can you?*

I'd spent years mocking Jackie's OCD *washers*. "What a bunch of freaks," I'd say about them, never suspecting for a second that I would someday join their ranks, scrubbing my hands under scalding water until I could bear it no more.

The handwashers I'd always read about tended to obsess about picking up someone else's deadly germs. Not me. My all too predictable concern was that I'd kill off everyone around me with some virulent plague I might unknowingly be carrying. Still, when it came to *how* we'd tackle our obsessions, the traditional washers and I had very similar approaches: (1) Do whatever it takes to get and keep our hands clean; and (2) Avoid direct contact with other people unless absolutely necessary. Unfortunately, the latter of these rules-to-live-by presented some monumental challenges for someone in a profession in which community appearances play such a large role.

Remote broadcasts. Speaking engagements. Client dinners. Everywhere I'd go, someone was always sticking a hand out my way. For a while, I was fine if I could just scrub up before the handshaking started, but after watching some guy in a reception line sneeze into his hand and then shake mine a few minutes later, the rules grew that much more stringent. From then on, to avoid spreading germs from one stranger to another, I'd have to shun *consecutive* handshakes. Or get creative with the pocket-sized bottle of hand sanitizer that I'd taken to carrying with me at absolutely all times:

"I'm Steve," some guy would say, extending his hand in my general direction. "I listen to you and Kitty every afternoon."

"Uh, thanks, Steve," I'd mutter. "I'll be with you in just *one* second."

And then the real challenge would begin. While turning my back to him (as if taking care of something), I'd shove my right hand into my pocket, opening my little bottle of Purell and squeezing a drop of the goo into my palm. Swinging back around, I'd use my left hand to rub in the lotion, and if all went as planned, I'd have protected us both. Of course, when circumstances didn't allow for my magic act, I could, and did, opt for my backup plan—lying:

"Hey Steve, nice to meet you," I'd say. "Please forgive my lack of manners, but I've got ink on my hands." Or I'd say peanut butter or salsa or anything sticky. Worked like a charm.

The remarkable thing about my elaborate double life in Sacramento is that I managed to pull it off so well. A full eighteen months I went with nary a soul knowing about my secret world of obsessions and compulsions. No one—not even Kitty, who shared a studio with me for three hours a day—had any clue about my laundry list of hang-ups and quirks. Not a solitary new blemish had I allowed on my permanent record since arriving at KFBK.

But on a Tuesday morning in late April 1997 this is about to change. I have called our minister, Wayne Manning, out of desperation, really, having summarily dismissed Jackie many months before, conceding to myself that I wasn't even trying anymore to do her assignments. I'm guessing there's not a whole lot Wayne can do to help me with my new germ concerns or any of my other OCD issues, but that's okay. I've got an even bigger challenge for him. After writing off every form of psychological and medical support made available to me, I know I'm now close to doing something similar with all things spiritual, including the Believer tag I'm so tempted to yank off my neck in a final surrender to Doubt's taunting about my pathetic hypocrisy.

If Wayne thinks he can talk me out of doing so, well, I figure I really ought to let him try.

■

"Is that all I have to accomplish in the next sixty minutes?"

Wayne deadpans the question after hearing me spell out the purpose of my visit and learning that it's now up to him to keep me from turning my back on God forever.

"I'm thinking you might need more than one hour," I concede.

"I'm yours for as long as you want me," Wayne says, and I know that he means it. The two of us have become casual friends over the past year or so, and during that time, I've seen his genuine compassion make a huge difference in a whole lot of lives. A former Army man with post-military experience in at least a half dozen fields, Wayne is a roll-up-the-sleeves kind of guy, a minister who practices what he preaches—which at a Unity church is a gospel of "applied spirituality." If anyone can dispense any practical advice on sacred matters, I'm certain that it's Wayne.

"So where do you want to begin?" he asks.

The million-dollar question. I haven't a clue.

"Well, for starters," I say, "there's a lot you don't know about me, Wayne."

"Okay. How 'bout you give me *the rest of the story.*"

Wayne's choice of words is a deliberate reference to Paul Harvey's *The Rest of the Story* feature, which runs during my show every afternoon. Wayne is a diehard KFBK listener and a former radio guy himself—facts greatly compounding the discomfort I'm feeling at this particular moment.

"Hmmm. . . okay, well, I . . . uh . . . have this thing, this anxiety disorder . . . something called OCD." I spit out the words like olive pits, then bumble my way through an overview of all the basics—my obsessions, my compulsions, the tape reviews (real and virtual), and so on—along with a detailed recap of my treatment history.

Wayne keeps his eyes locked on mine, and I see in them a growing pool of confusion. I know what I'm confessing here has got to be coming at him from deep in left field. Like the rest of our listeners who drive home with me every afternoon, Wayne has come to know the guy on my cassette airchecks, the normal one who's got his act together.

"So there you have it," I say when I can think of nothing else to explain.

"Wow."

Wow? This brilliant Sunday morning orator can

preach for hours on end, and *Wow* is all he can come up with for me after I bare every cubic inch of my soul? I have left him speechless.

"Pretty bizarre, eh?" I say, just to break the silence.

"Unbelievable. Never in million years would I have guessed you were dealing with all that."

Wayne asks me a whole series of questions next, and I do my best to answer them. I hold nothing back. I put it all out there in one big ugly pile. When our hour is about up, Wayne tells me he feels entirely unqualified to offer any clinical suggestions regarding OCD, but that he's very curious to learn why I'm convinced there's no room for God in my obsessive-compulsive world. We make plans to pick up our conversation the following Friday.

         ■

"It's the damn Twelve Steps," I inform Wayne in the opening minutes of our second meeting.

"The Twelve Steps?" he says, again looking deep into my eyes, as if perhaps I'm stashing some rational explanations in the back of my head.

"Right. Steps eight and nine, as I recall."

"The making of amends," Wayne says without missing a beat. As a Unity minister, he is more than familiar with AA's pragmatic approach to spiritual recovery.

"Yep, good old-fashioned amends-making. My OCD is having a field day with that whole concept."

Wayne's a sharp guy. I can almost see his brain connecting all the dots as I continue to explain things: "One of the steps involves making a list of all the people you've harmed—"

"And the other involves making direct amends to those people wherever possible," Wayne interrupts, eyes closed, face raised to the ceiling.

"I guess all that makes sense for a recovering alcoholic," I say. "But, man, in the hands of an obsessive-compulsive who's convinced that he's harmed every person who ever crossed his path, steps eight and nine are a brutal one-two punch."

Wayne nods his head. "Your Step Eight list is a long one, I'm willing to bet."

"You have no idea," I say, trying to keep myself from falling apart in yet another therapist's office. "All that mental reviewing I do in the middle of the night, it's all about checking and double-checking my list, making sure there's not a single person I'm forgetting to include."

"And what exactly is it that you want to 'make good' with all these people?"

Another tough one. How do I explain the whole parallel to scrubbing my hands till I'm certain they're sterile? "I guess I just want to fix everything. Restore perfection to my moral record."

"Your moral record?"

"Yeah, Samantha accuses me of running for Messiah."

Wayne likes this and laughs. He then suggests we try tackling a specific example. I pick a minor car accident I was involved in back in the late '80s and explain how the circumstances were such that it was unclear who was actually to blame, and how I'd made a comment suggesting as much at the time of the mishap. Days later, though, when it came down to who would pay for what, I played hardball as I'd always been taught—even denying that I'd implied at first that we were both to blame. This other guy thought we should each pay for our own damages; I, having convinced myself that the mishap was all his fault, insisted *he* pay for everything.

"So what happened?" Wayne asks.

"My insurance company chose not to push the issue and we wound up taking care of our own expenses, just as he'd suggested."

"Afraid I lost you, then. Where's the problem?"

I try to describe for Wayne how my black-and-white world works. How, for years, my taunting *what-if?* thoughts have raised a variety of possible horrors that might have happened because I recanted my initial comments about mutual blame.

"So what is it you feel compelled to do?"

"Track this guy down and tell him he was

right—we probably *were* both responsible, and, yes, I had implied so that day—and I'm so sorry for having been such a prick about everything."

"Two questions," Wayne says, holding up a pair of fingers. "One: would it change anything now? And two: for whose benefit do you want to do this?"

"Well, *no*. And *mine*, I suppose," I mutter in reply. "But all these damn spiritual books I'm reading, even your lessons Sunday after Sunday—they keep suggesting I need to confront my mistakes."

"Yeah, but I think you might be missing the—" Wayne interrupts himself and says nothing for a good couple of seconds, almost as if he's trying to tap into some invisible reservoir of inspiration he keeps in the room. "Okay, here's the deal," he finally says. "I want you to have that conversation you're longing to have. Tell this guy everything you want to say. Listen to his replies. But do it all *on paper*. And just for good measure, toss in a few lines for God, whom we'll pretend is there and taking part in your chat."

■

It takes me days to get past the first sentence of my little homework assignment. The whole exercise strikes me as a supreme waste of time, and I put it off again and again. When I finally do sit down at my word processor, I want to put the most venomous words possible in the mouth of my accident neme-sis, make him hate me for all the pain and suffering I imagine I've caused him over the years. But I can't. Not with my God character standing right there, tak-ing part in our conversation. Instead what comes out on my paper is an almost tearful reunion of two guys who come to understand that their seemingly chance meeting was no accident at all, that it played out for some greater good, and that only its lessons are worth hanging on to anymore.

This is all a bit too weird for me. But with each word I write, that much more of my guilt slips right off my shoulders like thick layers of melting snow sliding down a sloped roof in the first sunshine to follow a storm.

I share this with Wayne the following morning when we get together in his office. He congratulates me and suggests I take note of what this feels like to truly let go. To forgive and be forgiven. To put the past be-hind you. To repent, in the truest sense of the word.

Now I am breaking down again and I don't even know why. The only sound I can hear is that of my own hysterics. Wayne's not one to waste his words on hollow, feel-good BS, so he lets me get this out of my system.

I am embarrassed, though. Horribly embar-rassed. I've fallen apart in front of plenty of thera-pists before, so that's not the issue. Nor is coming unglued in the company of my minister. But Wayne, in my mind at this moment, is neither a shrink nor a clergyman. He is simply a loyal KFBK listener, one whose image of me is forever shattered.

"I know there's a reason for this," I whisper at last, pointing my index fingers inward at this pathetic figure balled up on the couch. "I know it's all part of God's plan for me."

Silence. Nothing from Wayne. I can hear him breathing in a nearby chair.

"Someday," I say, "I'm going to conquer this beast. And when I do, I'm going to have quite a story to tell. And I *am* going to tell that story."

Good God, where did that come from?

And what was that in my voice? Confidence? Certainty? Resolve? Conviction?

I feel a hand on my shoulder now. Hear Wayne clearing his throat, about to say something.

"You *do* know, don't you, that you're writing that book right now?"

Yeah, right, I laugh to myself, thinking about the hours it takes me to write and rewrite, check and recheck, and again write and rewrite, a simple news script at the station. I can only imagine what Doubt would do with a full-length manuscript covering a subject so wrought with uncertainty, a subject I'm already regretting having brought up with anyone.

seventeen

fast-forward 3 weeks

I suppose I should have seen this coming, should have anticipated the inevitable backlash. Doubt doesn't like me conjuring up hopeful images of the future, not even for just a few minutes as I somehow managed to do in Wayne Manning's office. Now there is hell to pay, and Doubt is collecting from high atop a director's chair, barking *Take that!* through a megaphone, plotting new and twisted ways to cast me as a villain, and stealing script ideas from the very news stories I read day after day. It's the same little trick that led me from that news item about hepatitis C to countless hours of hand-scrubbing ever since.

The pattern soon becomes all too familiar. One afternoon, Kitty and I do a story about a house burning down because of dead batteries in a smoke detector, and that night, I lie awake reviewing tapes of every house and apartment in which I ever lived. *Did I leave any of their smoke detectors inoperable or without fully charged batteries?* Another afternoon we cover an embezzlement story, and hours later in bed, I toss and turn my way through tape after tape spanning years' worth of jobs. *Did I ever fail to return company property—binders, reference books, rulers, anything?*

And so it goes day after day, week after week, until Doubt grinds me down and leaves me defenseless. I have no fight left in me, none, when yet another freeway episode from my distant past grabs hold of me, so I start looking for relief at any cost.

I come up with a plan. If I can just have a peek at this stretch of Highway 280 (more than a hundred miles from home), *then* I can figure things out and be done for good with this entire mess.

"That's a trap, and you know it," Samantha tells me, when I run the idea by her. "We've been through this before. So many times!"

"This one's different," I protest.

"You say that about all of them."

"I just don't know what else to do."

"Go back and see Wayne."

"No. We had closure," I say. "We wrapped up our sessions on such a positive note. I don't want to go messing with that."

Samantha can't understand this. "Okay," she says, "then give Jackie a call."

"Too awkward. I pretty much sent her packing the last time we talked."

"Fine. Then *you* come up with a plan."

"I did," I remind her. "That's why I want to call in sick tomorrow and go to the Bay Area."

Sam is running out of patience with me. As of late, her pity and compassion are turning to frustration and anger. I know she's feeling helpless. Or worse yet, ignored.

"Okay, I'll call Jackie," I finally concede. I say it as if I'm doing her a favor, when in fact I know it's the other way around.

Jackie and I talk for an hour the following morning. Like a home-cooked meal after weeks on the road, our conversation reminds me of what it is I've been missing. The firm coaching. The frank talk. The familiarity of it all. We cover the old freeway incident and my new obsession with making amends. We talk about coping strategies. By the time our session is over, I'm ready to get things back on track, to talk on the phone on a regular basis. But Jackie tells me we've exhausted that route, that what I really need now is someone I can see in person. She knows a guy in Sacramento.

His name is Dr. Z, and I surprise myself by making and keeping an appointment with him. Nice man. Great credentials. Knows his stuff inside and out. But by the time we wrap up our first session, I know I can't do this again. Can't start all over with yet another shrink. My head's just not in it, which I suppose is the crux of the problem.

■

A week later, I am implementing my original plan. I win. Sam loses. And she loses big, since she is the one driving me down Highway 280, once each direction past my point of concern, as the two of us negotiated after another drawn-out debate over what I need as a matter of survival.

"That's all you get," Sam says, just before looking over at me and nearly gasping when she sees what I'm doing.

"*What?*" I say, trying to downplay the fact that I have a video camera in my hand and am taping the freeway and everything around it. I need to get all this on tape, so I can play on my VCR what I'm already playing endlessly in my head.

It turns out my taping skills were atrocious. The video I managed to capture at 65 miles per hour is hardly helpful. Blurry, bouncy shots, mostly ob-scured by objects in the car and my own two hands. Still I play, rewind, and replay the Super-8 tape again and again, searching for any clues I might have missed before, much as I continue to do with my vir-tual tapes in the middle of the night.

Life is growing darker around the edges with each passing day. More fear. More guilt. More shame. And more bitterness. "Why me?" I catch myself whispering night after night. Why do *I* have to spend my life checking and rechecking, review-ing and re-creating? Why do *I* have to run around in the shadows hiding from kids and the homeless and potholes and germs? Why do *I* have to drive in circles and scrub my hands and call my wife every ten minutes? No one else I know seems to have these burdens. What have *I* done to deserve this liv-ing hell?

Shall we review? Doubt is right there, as always, with an editorial reply.

■

"How 'bout you call this Dr. Schwartz?" Samantha asks me one afternoon in mid-August, nearly two full months after my old freeway obsessions began.

Sam is referring to Dr. Jeffrey Schwartz, a UCLA psychiatrist and author of the most recent OCD book the two of us have read. It's called *Brain Lock,* and it offers what's billed as a four-step self-treatment program for struggling OCs.

Schwartz's approach is similar to traditional cognitive behavioral therapy, with a couple of key distinctions. First, he introduces the concept of mindful awareness, encouraging OCs to make use of their own internal "Impartial Spectator," to step back and see that their intrusive thoughts and irrational urges are simply obsessions and compulsions caused by a biochemical imbalance. And second, Schwartz advocates that OCs actively *refocus* their attention on something more constructive while trying to work around their persistent thoughts—play a game, prune plants in the garden, those kinds of things.

I like these tactics because they strike me as especially consistent with Jerry Jampolsky's dueling directors model that I've been trying to use. Director Doubt is nothing more than my OCD, with a biological basis to boot. And as for the refocusing, isn't that what Jampolsky's young cancer patients have so successfully learned to do with their thoughts and attention?

"I'm serious. I think you should call him," Samantha repeats.

"Dr. Schwartz?"

"Yeah."

"Right. The guy's been on *Oprah*, *Leeza*, and

Extra. He's really gonna have time to chat with me on the phone?"

"And you've got something to lose in trying?" Sam says. Or read between the lines: *With Jackie and Wayne and that local guy out of the mix, who else are you going to turn to as you fall apart a little more every day?*

I make the call, just to prove to Samantha that I'm right, that a guy in Schwartz's league is inaccessible to someone like me.

It turns out though that I'm wrong about this. Not only does Dr. Jeffrey Schwartz return my call, he also agrees to set up a time when the two of us can discuss my challenges. We make plans to chat on August 26 at 7:30 p.m.

At 7:29:30 on the designated evening I pick up the phone and call Dr. Schwartz's L.A. number. Our conversation starts out just fine. I run though the basics of my particular obsessions and compulsions, and Schwartz assures me that my OCD patterns are rather typical. We talk for a while about his Four Step approach and how I'm trying to apply it, and then I decide to go for broke: What the hell, I'm going to get my money's worth here and have this international authority put an end, once and for all, to my freeway incident. All I need is some comment like "Oh, that's just your OCD" or "You do realize, don't you, that this whole thing is all a bunch of garbage?" and chances are Doubt's spell will be broken. I know I managed to sandbag Jackie a time or two with similar reassurance ploys—that is, until she called me on the carpet for what I was doing.

But Schwartz doesn't bite when I launch into my story. Occasional questions are all he offers along the way. Maybe he too is onto my little checking game.

Or maybe he's thinking that I've done something truly horrible!

Time runs out before I know it, and we arrange to pick things up one week from tonight. The phone receiver is shaking in my hand as I put it back in its cradle. My anxiety level is through the roof. It's as if my brain is a cross-wired capacitor with no circuitry in place to discharge its current; any minute now the whole thing's going to fry.

For almost an hour I hole up in the living room, replaying tonight's phone conversation in my head again and again. Samantha checks in on me, hoping to hear that her latest suggestion has proved to be a good one. Instead she finds me rocking back and forth on the couch, keeping time with my body to Schwartz's looping voice in my head.

"I take it your chat didn't go so well?" Sam's disappointment is written all over her face.

"I don't know. All I can think about is how

I presented the freeway incident and whether Schwartz thinks I am guilty."

"That's ridiculous," Sam says. "Ludicrous. Jeff—"

"I dunno. It's all so boggled in my head. I just wish we'd had more time."

Sam checks her watch. "Call him back and see if he can talk for a few more minutes." My wife wants so badly for this to work. For *something* to work.

I twist her comment around. I take it to mean that she too feels I need to convince Schwartz that there never was any real issue with the whole incident. That I am innocent.

Samantha goes to put the girls to bed. I pick up the phone.

"Dr. Schwartz? It's Jeff Bell again. I know it's late, but can I have just a *little* more of your time?"

Thirty minutes later I hang up the receiver a second time and again begin reviewing the call in my head. I am feeling much better about the whole guilt-or-innocence thing. That's no longer an issue. But now there is something else: a clearly sarcastic crack Schwartz made about some argument I was using as being "the kind that leads patients to a hospital stay," or something like that.

A hospital stay?!

He was just being sarcastic, I remind myself. He was just trying to make a point about illogical reasoning. I try to focus on all the positive, constructive suggestions Schwartz had offered.

But it's too late. The words *hospital stay* have begun bouncing around my head, electronic pings like those of the old Pong video games.

Hospital-*stay*. Hospital-*stay*. Hospital-*stay*.

Soon I am in our master bathroom, rifling through all the drawers in the vanity, scrambling to find my old bottle of pills. Nearly nine months have passed since I stashed my remaining blue tablets somewhere in this room, promising myself that I'd never again become a slave to their power.

But what choice do I have? I need to whip myself into shape in a hurry. Before the men in white suits show up at my doorstep and haul me away for a *hospital stay*. I know OCs aren't supposed to take medication without supervision. But I can't wait for Dr. Schwartz or Jackie or any other professional to put me on some official drug program. The clock is ticking. *Where are my damn pills?*

"Sam?"

She is in bed, half awake if even that.

"I need to find my pills," I whisper. "I'm going back on meds."

No sound from the bed. I'm not sure the news has even registered. But I wonder, because on Samantha's sleeping face there's now a hint of a smile.

I continue to fumble in the drawers. *Come on. Come on. Before I change my mind.*

Finally. At the far back of the second drawer down, I feel a plastic bottle and pull it out where I can read the label.

Zoloft. Fifty milligrams. Take only as directed.

I know it's Doubt *directing* me next as I close my eyes, open my mouth, and take this all too powerful pill that I'm certain is either going to save my life or end it right here.

eighteen

fast-forward 30 minutes

Of all the tape segments in my archives, the handful spanning the next twenty-four hours have a unique distinction: they're the only ones with their own movie score. Pianos. Violins. Loud, resonant organ chords. Overblown music to punctuate the string of soap opera sequences that make up these classics.

Time has messed with my recordings of these crucial hours, quite possibly giving them more significance than they ought to have. And yet to this day I can think of no more dramatic scenes from my life than the ones that begin here, with me curled up in a ball on the living room couch, knees tucked to my chest, arms wrapped tightly around them . . .

Numb me, damn it, numb me. For God's sake, please, I beg of you, numb me.

At least a half-hour now I have spent balled up and waiting. Nothing. No effects whatsoever from the little blue pill I have swallowed. Not even with all of my pleading. I know the benefits of Zoloft can take up to six weeks to kick in, but I haven't got that long; I need relief *now*. I also know that Zoloft is not a "numbing" drug—like the ones the serious nut-cases take in the movies—but it's the only drug I've got at my disposal, and I'm certain that numbing is what I need at this moment, so numbing is what I beg for as I slowly come to accept the real reason I have dug out my dusty bottle of pills.

Still nothing.

I pass the time the way I always do, playing and replaying the OCD horror films that Doubt demands I review. There are so many tapes to cue up tonight, and ultimately, I fast-forward each to the same bitter end, to that familiar final scene at the virtual mad-house I've been visiting ever since Jackie first led me there nearly three years ago.

With the words *hospital stay* still pinging back and forth between my ears, I imagine myself in a small, blinding white cell on a generic psych ward, waiting for Samantha and the girls to arrive for their weekly visit, and pleading with my hospital medication to further numb me from the pain of my plight and all the tapes I continue to loop in my head. The images grow ever more vivid and disturbing as I slip into and out of the fantasy time and again, always embellishing on the basic scene I'd first conjured up for Jackie in her little exposure-therapy exercise.

Jackie. I think about her now and all the years we spent together. So many breakthroughs and successes and triumphs big and small. So much genuine progress earned over so many hours of gut-wrenching therapy. And yet in the end, *this* is where it all got me: a fetal-position breakdown on my living room couch. Damn you, Jackie, for failing to fix me.

Dr. X.

Dr. Y.

Dr. Z.

Dr. Smith.

Dr. Schwartz.

Reverend Manning.

Damn all of you, too, for coming up short.

But most of all, damn *you,* you lousy piece-of-shit pill, for failing to numb me.

The night wears on and an ugly reality sinks in: as terrifying as my nuthouse fantasy might be, it is also somehow perversely alluring to me. That's why

Schwartz's sarcastic quip about hospitalization is still ringing in my ears—because some part of me *wants* to hear it. Because the cruel truth of the matter is I *want* to be in the hospital cell I can see in my mind, sheltered safely from society and all my friends and relatives and colleagues and listeners who just assume I am normal. And this, I now understand, is why I swallowed the pill—because in my black-and-white obsessive-compulsive world, choosing to take my little Zoloft tablet is tantamount to checking myself into a mental institution, retreating to the one place in the world where I can finally put an end to my elaborate charade of normalcy and accept my lot in life as a rank-and-file member of the mentally ill.

Five years. Six therapists. Two medications. Hundreds, maybe thousands, of OCD episodes. Countless hours of excruciating tape reviews. I have had enough. I want out. And so, at long last, I allow myself to finally quit the fight, to let all the exhaustion shut me down, right here on the couch.

Now I *am* numb, inside and out, as I advance my very worst horror film to its final few frames: Sam and the girls are in the hallway just outside my hospital cell, mere inches away from their first sight of me as a pathetic drugged-up lunatic. Brianna is crying as they step up to the doorway . . .

"No! Stop the tape!" I scream the words silently

at the brink of my last waking moment, a single heartbeat before something deep inside of me gently begins to whisper:

This isn't the way. This can't be the way.

■

I open my eyes and it's morning now. I am still curled up on the living room couch, but the very walls that had morphed themselves into an asylum cell around me last night are now open canvases for silhouettes of flowers and birds shaped by the slants of sunshine beaming through our sliding glass window. Sam and the girls are nowhere in sight, and the house is so quiet it's eerie. Stranger still is the rare silence inside my head, the distinct absence of Doubt's thundering presence. And oddest of all is the *timing* of my newfound peace. I'm certain it's not the result of six hours of sleep, and I refuse to accept that it's the byproduct of a mere fifty milligrams of Zoloft.

The utter stillness unnerves me at first. I imagine Doubt hiding at its edges, waiting to ambush me at just the right moment, as it's done so many times before during the hush of a pitch black night or the sacred silence of prayer. For some reason though, I find myself feeling especially bold. I decide to go for it, to climb inside the silence, to see where it takes me.

Breathe in. *Let God*. Breathe out. *Let go*. Breathe in. *Let God*. Breathe out. *Let go*.

This is the way all my books say to do it.

Breathe in. *Let God*. Breathe out. *Let go*.

A deep blue spot takes form in the center of my mind's eye. It grows and grows in pulsating waves. I try to focus my attention on it and block out everything else.

Breathe in. *Let God*. Breathe out. *Let go*.

Soon there is just blue and the sound of my breaths. No *what-if's* to ponder. No tapes to play. No OCD monsters of any kind to feed. No words to describe the bliss of this freedom.

Seconds pass, or are they hours?

And then I get it: This is the *now*. The *present*. That infinite slice of time wedged between the past and the future.

It is the place of unlimited, unfathomable possibility, and because of this, it is the one place Doubt cannot exist.

Suddenly everything begins to make sense. For five interminable years from hell, my nemesis has steered me clear of each and every precious moment of my present, feeding me one compelling cause after another to obsess about my future while compulsively reviewing tapes of my past.

Rewind. Play. Fast-forward. Rewind. Play. Fast-forward. Day after day, I've been locked in this cycle, entirely incapable of ever getting out.

I've read enough to know the power of free will exists only in the present. Choices simply cannot be made in the past or future. And this, I decide, is precisely why Doubt loves to lead me right from yesterday's mistakes to tomorrow's catastrophes, leaving me no time at all to take control of my life.

It's a vicious cycle.

And yet there *was* that profound quiet voice last night that was trying to . . .

"Hello. Thanks for calling. We're not home right now. If you'd like to leave a message . . . ." The moment is gone, disappearing along with the pulsating blue spot at the *Beeep* of our answering machine.

I open my eyes, almost relieved to be back in the mundane world of telephones and voice mail. I have again pushed the borders of my fledgling spirituality way beyond my personal comfort zone.

But the notion of free will haunts me as I sit on the couch and stare out the window at nothing in particular. I think about a diagram I once saw in a Stephen Covey book that was meant to show the key distinction between humans and other species. There were two boxes, one marked "Stimulus" on the left, one labeled "Response" to its right, and in between them the words "Freedom to Choose." I think about the diagram now, and I think about Jerry Jampolsky's "dueling directors" model, and I think about Dr. Schwartz's "impartial spectators" and refocusing techniques.

There's an obvious theme here, and it's anything but lost on me as my mind moves next to the parade of therapists who tried to help me. How many times did I catch myself waiting for one of them to wave a magic wand and make me all better? How many dire reminders did Jackie offer that my progress would only come when I was willing to do the hard work, to make the tough choices? How many pills did I take for all the wrong reasons—to numb myself, instead of to help make me stronger?

But all that's in the past. I am now living in the present. This moment is rife with possibility and potential. Unfortunately, it's also a good half hour after I was supposed to leave the house. I'll have to pick up my unusually lucid thinking tonight.

I am on a roll, and I know it. Plato has nothing on me.

■

Some ten hours later, I sprawl out in a backyard hammock beneath a bazillion stars overhead. It's a sticky August night and a chorus of crickets is about the only sound I can hear. I am more excited and invigorated than I can remember being in years, and I'm not too sure I understand why.

I do the breathing thing again, but it gets me no-where this time. No blue spots or pulsating waves, so I just open my eyes and stare upward until I lose myself in a flickering star.

Soon I am again contemplating the power of free will, fumbling with the *Believer* dog tag around my neck, thinking how true believing must involve the boldest of all choices, since when it comes right down to it, you're choosing to trust what you cannot see. I flash back to the handful of times in my life when I managed to do this—somehow put my faith in something bigger than myself—and I remember how powerful the results always were. I think about my old AA friends and all their tales about surren-dering their addictions to some Higher Power and coming to trust their own "greater good" guidance, and how they've used those inspiring stories to help so many others.

And then without any warning or logic, I catch myself making what feels like a bargain: *Okay, it's your turn,* I mouth upwards to the stars, unsure of just where to direct my pronouncement. *Show me how to turn around this crazy life, and I'll share my story with anyone who will listen.*

A strange sense of certainty washes over me next, and I know in this instant that nothing in my world will ever be the same. With a mixture of fear and excitement, I also come to realize that Wayne

Manning wasn't kidding with the last words he'd left me with in his office back in May.

For as preposterous as it strikes me at this moment, I now know I am indeed "writing that book."

nineteen

fast-forward 2 months

Day 1 (12:00 midnight). I stand now on the precipice of the most important undertaking of my life. This is it—my chance to put into motion the greatest premise of my belief: that I hold in my power the tools to transform. My outcome is certain or my premise eternally flawed.

I believe.

Precipice? Most important undertaking? Tools to transform? The words all sound so desperate, so dramatic, and mostly so foreign as I read them back to myself mere seconds after having committed them to paper. Yet here they are in my own handwriting, staring back at me from an index card—the first of hundreds I've stacked in an oversized shoe box just behind my desk. At this moment, the other cards in the box are all blank. Soon though, I tell myself, they will fill up with great wisdom and together take my life to new dimensions—three inches by five inches to be exact. Because for the next twelve months, three-by-five cards will indeed be at the very center of my world.

It's all part of my grand plan to *transform* my troubled life—that *most important undertaking* I've been plotting for nearly two months now, ever since my foolhardy "bargain with the stars" back in late August and my subsequent commitments to do all of the following: (1) reestablish contact with Jackie and arrange her coaching twice a month on the phone; (2) keep my little pills buried deep in a drawer until such time that I might actually need them for their *intended* purposes; (3) put myself back under the stars nightly for exactly one year, beginning tonight, on the eve of my thirty-fourth birthday; and (4) take notes, just in case I need to hold up my end of the bargain.

I have no idea whether I'll end up with a story to share, and therefore an obligation to share it. As a professional journalist, though, I do know a few things about note-taking, including the importance of always keeping with me a stash of index cards. On them I will record everything: all my obsessive thoughts, all my compulsive checking rituals, and all my triumphs and setbacks in dealing with both. I will fill out daily "journal cards" with all the observations I can make, and "episodes cards," detailing all the various OCD episodes with which I have to contend. I will take notes from the many books I've committed to read. And most of all, I will attempt to log and make sense of those occasional whispers coming not from my voice of doubt, but rather from some inner-believer I know is inside me—those very whispers that have led me to bank my entire future on a stack of empty three-by-five cards.

All this strikes me as both brilliant and ludicrous as I sit at my den desk at a little past midnight, no more than five minutes into my "project," as I have come to call it. I read back my scribbles one more time and shake my head as I reach the words *This is it.* Did I mean to do that, spell out the song title? I can't remember consciously doing so, but I guess I must have; the three words have been camped out in my head for sixteen years now—ever since that still-all-too-weird graduation speech experience and the last time I found myself sitting at a desk, staring at words so seemingly foreign.

This is it, all right, I whisper as I tuck the index card away in its new cardboard box home.

■

Morning arrives with a rousing chorus of "Happy Birthday to You." Samantha and the girls are singing to me from the bedroom doorway, and Nicole and Brianna are bouncing on their toes, the way kids do when they can contain their excitement no longer. The sight of my precious daughters and their mother all decked out in smiles and eager to greet me couldn't offer a more striking contrast to the final scene of my *Visiting Day at the Nuthouse* horror film, and I know that none of the gifts that they're holding could offer me more than this particular one.

The girls deliver their presents and hugs, then scurry off to get ready for school. Sam makes her way over to the bed and plants a kiss on my cheek.

"I can't remember the last time I saw *you* in such good spirits," she says.

"It's a big day," I tell her, wondering if she understands what I mean.

I've told Samantha about my journaling plans. But I've stopped far short of detailing the particulars of my full year-long project, and I haven't even hinted at the all-or-nothing stock I'm putting in it. It's a delicate subject with us, my recovery plans.

I've botched things so badly so many times. And though she'd never say so, I think Sam is disappointed with me for getting off my meds just as quickly as I'd gone back on them in August. Still, I know she's thrilled that I'm on a schedule with Jackie again.

The rest of the details can wait.

The girls leave the house an hour later, and I start putting together a survival kit of sorts that I plan to haul with me everywhere. I've dug out an old black leather notebook and I stuff it full of blank index cards, along with a pen. I also toss in a copy of an old "mission statement" I wrote some time back as part of a goal-setting exercise in a self-help book:

> To serve God in his chosen ways, while
>   demonstrating my belief:
> In myself, through integrity, strength,
>   initiative, and release;
> In others, through respect, compassion,
>   generosity, and trust;
> And in life, through passion, perspective,
>   involvement, and faith.
> All this and only this, right here and
>   right now.

The whole thing strikes me as rather over the top. In fact, for all my recent reading and practice during this stretch, spirituality continues to fit me like a coat at least three sizes too big. Still, the pragmatist in me understands how important a focal point is going to be in the months ahead, as I struggle to make this project the target of my ongoing refocusing efforts. So I promise myself I'll read over these words at least three times a day, every day, until next October 21.

And now I have everything I need. Index cards. My Believer dog tag. Self-help books to read on my breaks at work. Weekly goals from Jackie, just like old times. And a written reminder to do nothing more with my time than to *demonstrate* my belief— in myself, in others, and in life.

Yeah, good luck with all that, I can almost hear Doubt taunting.

■

At 9:30 I am out the door on my way to a production appointment, and a few minutes after that, I am attempting to get my little Mazda Protégé up to speed on the Forty-third Avenue on-ramp to northbound I-5. I am looking for a hole in the traffic now, battling my usual fears of cutting off cars and causing massive chain-reaction accidents, when I get this strange and sudden impulse to turn on my radio.

Huh?

The radio.

Oh, I get it, I say to myself. No way. I'm not playing that game. Compulsive urges are the calling cards of OCD. I've spent years fighting them, in all their disguises. That's what this is. A command from Doubt, no different from the usual ones to wash my hands or loop around the block or check my parking brake. Besides, there's a whole subset of OCD known as "magical thinking," and OCs who battle with it are always looking to draw meaning—and horrific conclusions—from the various mundane "signs" all around them. (Like whatever song might happen to be playing on the radio.)

But something is different, profoundly different, about this particular urge. It doesn't seem to suggest there will be any dire consequences if I fail to act on it. Perhaps just a missed opportunity. If for no other reason, I know this isn't Doubt egging me on. But then again, how many times in the past has my devious nemesis managed to trick me?

A few seconds pass, and then a few more. Still none of that familiar do-or-die pressure. Intense curiosity, in fact, is all that I'm feeling. I want there to be something good waiting for me. Finally I can take it no longer. I lunge for the On button and watch my jaw drop in the rearview mirror as my mind grasps what I am hearing. Blasting from my car speakers are the unmistakable opening chords of Kenny Loggins's "This Is It." Now the lyrics kick in, and for the first time in sixteen years, I truly *get* how powerful, and how ominous, their message is.

> *For once in your life, here's your miracle*
> *Stand up and fight*
> *This is it*
> *Make no mistake where you are*
> *This is it*
> *You're going no further*
> *This is it*
> *Until it's over and done*
> *. . . . This is it*
> *One way or another*

And then it hits me like a Mack truck barreling up from behind: what are the chances? I've always considered myself a student of commercial radio, and if there's one thing I'm certain of at this moment, it's that "This Is It" is not a song getting airplay in the late 1990s. It just isn't. I can't even remember the last time I heard it on our local airwaves. And of all the possible times and places to hear it now . . .

A shiver snaps to attention every hair on my body. This is not what I'd envisioned when I promised to "open myself to divine guidance," as Reverend Manning likes to put it. This has got to be some kind of OCD trap. Somehow, Doubt is messing with me.

An hour and a half later I am on the freeway again, now on my way to KFBK, when another urge starts tugging at me. This one, however, is both familiar and predictable in its timing. It begins the very second I swerve to avoid hitting a scrap of tire tread. *Get off at the next exit and loop back for a look. Check the shoulders for cars you may have hit in the process of swerving. Do it now, or people could die while waiting!*

This is Doubt. This time I'm sure. I will not give in.

I make it to the station parking lot without indulging my compulsion. But I pay the price big time as I walk from my car to the studio thinking about how irresponsible I am to have left the scene of yet another potential crash. I should go back—maybe on my lunch break. Perhaps I should call the highway patrol to report the small scrap of rubber. But it wasn't a very big scrap. *Or was it?* I play back a tape of the swerve as I continue crossing the parking lot. The usual fuzzy images are all I can make out. Damn it all. Can't I enjoy just one friggin' day?

And then I look down and see a nail on the ground.

Pick it up!

No.

Pick it up, or someone's going to get hurt.

No one's going to get hurt.

Pick it up, or some car is going to run over that nail and puncture its tire.

No. No! NO! I will not pick up the nail.

No?! What if that punctured tire causes a spin-out that kills lots of people?

All right, goddamn it. I'll pick up the nail.

I pick up the nail.

Oh, great! Now where you going to get rid of that lethal thing?

■

At ten that evening I am in our backyard, staring up at the stars, keeping the second of my 365 scheduled appointments with them. I have logged the nail and the tire-swerve on my "episodes" card for today and have done my best to recap the whole "This Is It" radio experience on today's journal cards. Now I'm just waiting for the Big Dipper or any other sparkling constellation up there to impart some great wisdom to me—to make sense of Day One of my project, or at a minimum to instruct me to turn on my television, or open the freezer, or look in my dresser sock drawer for more inspiration like I found on the radio.

Nothing.

It was just a damn coincidence, that song, you big loser. Get over it, says the voice in my head.

twenty

fast-forward 1 day

Richard Dreyfuss in *Close Encounters of the Third Kind*.

That's me in my next tape-segment starring role. Listen, and you can almost hear that haunting five-note sequence: G . . . A . . . F . . . F . . . C . . .

The segment starts off so innocently, really. There I am, sitting in my parked car after the Noon News, reciting my mission statement for the ump-teenth time on Project Day Two, mulling over the un-canny symmetry of the twelve words I'd chosen several years back to define my goals in believing:

> . . . in myself, through integrity, strength,
> initiative, and release.
> . . . in others, through respect, compas-
> sion, generosity, and trust.
> . . . in life, through passion, perspective,
> involvement, and faith.

And then it dawns on me, much as solutions to complex math problems suddenly make themselves clear, or once-elusive answers to riddles become obvious in an instant: rearrange the words and stack them in a pyramid.

So that's what I do. Grab a pair of index cards from my notebook, and urgently sketch out top and side views: one side *Self*; a second side *Others*; and the third side *Life*. Then, starting from the base and working toward its apex, I give my three-sided pyramid four horizontal tiers (which I would later label *Reverence, Resolve, Investment,* and *Surrender.*)

Finally, I drop my twelve words into place.

There are few things in life more satisfying to an obsessive-compulsive than a solid sense of order. Perhaps this is why I find myself speechless as I gaze at the crude drawing I've just made. The symmetry. The associative groupings. The spatial relationships. A perfect model of the inner structure of belief. I can't wait to finish up my shift at the station and get home to build a mockup. For three long

"Structure of Belief" Pyramid

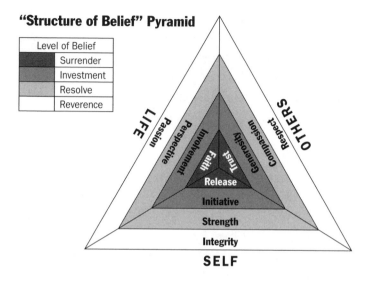

Level of Belief
Surrender
Investment
Resolve
Reverence

LIFE
Passion
Perspective
Involvement
Faith
Release
Trust
Compassion
Generosity
Respect
OTHERS
Initiative
Strength
Integrity
SELF

hours on the air, I talk about homicides and interest rates and the Kings' next big game, all the while thinking about one and only one thing: pyramids.

Once home, I begin mulling over construction options, and that's when the whole Richard Dreyfuss thing kicks in. Remember that dinner-table scene in which his character becomes obsessed with some illusory mountain shape? He needs to give it form, so he does what any quick-thinking diner would do: he starts sculpting his mashed potatoes.

Samantha's not serving potatoes or anything else malleable this particular night, so I power-eat my dinner and quickly excuse myself to the den, where I start cutting up cardboard. For the next several hours, I sit at my desk folding cardboard into pyramids of all sizes, giving three dimensions to the geometric shape taking up all the space in my head. By the time I climb into bed, I have put the finishing touches on a three-inch model with all twelve of my believing words stenciled neatly in their places.

II PAUSE Okay, you already know I'm nuts. I think I've made that abundantly clear. But I can only imagine what you're thinking right about now. I mean, here's this guy who's talking to the stars at night, gleaning divine messages from his car radio, and now stamping out cardboard pyramids. Pretty damn weird, even for an admitted obsessive-compulsive who drives his car in circles, scrubs his hands till they hurt, and checks and rechecks everything around him. But here's the craziest part of it all: that three-inch cardboard pyramid, the one I crafted that night and that sits on my desk to this day, still strikes me as the sanest, most rational, truest thing I have ever seen.

I dunno. Maybe OCD is just the beginning of my psychosis.

► PLAY Trust. Strength. Faith . . .
Four days after building my cardboard mockup, I am at our church, mentally scrambling to affix my believing words to their proper places on

the virtual pyramid I have etched in my mind. The woman extending her hand to me while I'm attempting to do this is making the process exceptionally tricky.

"You must be Jeff Bell," she says, smiling.

She looks pretty normal, this woman. Composed. Dignified, in fact, with elegant features, perfectly coiffed silver hair and a big, light-up-the-room smile that reminds me at once of actress Andie MacDowell's.

Maybe this isn't the woman I'd agreed to meet today. I'm expecting a freak.

"My husband and I listen to you all the time," she continues, waiting for me to say something. Anything.

A listener. Wouldn't that just figure? I knew this was a bad idea. I'm supposed to emcee the Sacramento Ballet's matinee this afternoon, and I'm already uptight about that. I don't need this added anxiety. I want to bolt. Unfortunately, a quick assessment tells me that's no longer an option.

Integrity. Initiative. Generosity . . .

"And you must be Carole Johnson," I finally say, opting to acknowledge this woman before I become the one who looks like a freak. "Wayne speaks very highly of you."

Wayne Manning has been after me for months to get together with Carole. "She's written a book you might find interesting," he's told me, hinting that Carole shares some of the quirky habits I'd copped to during our sessions last spring. What made me finally agree to meet her today, on Day Six of my project, though, I can't imagine.

Church is letting out, and the two of us are standing in the foyer, midstream in a rising tide of people.

"How 'bout we find someplace quiet to talk?" I whisper to Carole.

Walking down the hall I remind myself how carefully I've kept my secret, how I can still count on my fingers and toes the total number of people who know about my little problem, and how this built-in cap seems like the perfect limit for such private matters. I think about all the years I spent paying for expensive therapy out of my own pocket to avoid a health-care paper trail, how I slithered into and out of one shrink's office after another to escape getting caught. Why on earth would I now risk my entire radio career on a stranger, no matter how much that stranger and I might have in common?

We find a place to tuck away, and Carole hands me a copy of her self-published book.

"It's an autobiography," she says. "But there are a number of local tie-ins you might be interested in."

I stare at her, confused, for a second or two before it hits me: she thinks I'm meeting her to arrange an author interview for my show. That's how Wayne must have pitched it. She hasn't a clue. I'm home free. My secret is safe. I open my mouth, prepare to give her my producer's name and phone number.

But then something happens, something I'm entirely unprepared for. Our eyes meet and lock, and I see in hers a reflection of my own. The pain. The fear. The embarrassment. The desperation. All the indescribably debilitating by-products of a life spent chasing the demands of a hiccupping brain. All of it right there, hidden in a pair of sparkling brown eyes fooling the entire world except for a select few like me, who from years of shared horrors, can somehow see clear through the façade.

It's all so overwhelming, standing here face to face with another member of my rare and unspoken-of species. People are squeezing by us now in the narrow hallway. I should say something, move us off to the side. But I can't move.

"I . . . I do what you do," I hear myself stutter as Carole wraps her arms around me. Quite clearly, I need not explain what I mean by my confession.

"I know, Jeff," she whispers in my ear. "I know. And now that we've found each other, we'll never again have to suffer through all this alone."

Something about the intimacy and vulnerability of the moment scares me. And yet at this same moment, I know this: every bit as much as my index cards and my mission statement and my pyramid model and my dog tag and Jackie's regular guidance, Carole Johnson is going to play a huge role in my project. That she'd prove to have invisible wings and a halo, I'm not sure I yet knew.

twenty-one

fast-forward 4 days

Day Ten, 6:55 p.m. Kitty and I are about to wrap up the KFBK Afternoon News. It's been a good show. Good news mix, good guests, good call-in segments. After two years together, the two of us are really meshing as an anchor team. Solid shows like today's are now routine.

I love this job. And as I look around the studio, I realize what a refuge this little room has become for me. No matter how horrific the day's OCD episodes might be, if I can just make it into this studio, I'm always home free. Here I am what I am paid to be: poised, confident, in control. The guy our listeners ride home with is as normal as normal gets. Even Kitty is still oblivious to the many ramifications of my malfunctioning brain. I suppose that in fooling all of them day after day, I'm somehow managing to fool myself in the process.

Tomorrow is a big day. The station is cohosting an international speakers' symposium called *Perspectives '97*, and Kitty and I are scheduled to introduce legendary television anchorman David Brinkley to the crowd. Brinkley has long been one of my news heroes, so the prospect of meeting him one-on-one has me counting the minutes to the end of the show, when I can head home and begin prepping for our chat.

At seven I crack the mic one more time and close out our program: "KFBK, Sacramento. It's . . . seven o'clock."

ABC takes over the airwaves with the network's hourly newscast and Kitty and I pack up our stuff. We make plans to meet in the morning just before the symposium. We've got our scripts. Everything is in place.

Heading for the door, I hear someone in the newsroom shout, "Hey Jeff, your wife's on line one." I don't know why, but I get a knot in my gut.

"We have a problem," Samantha tells me as soon as I pick up the phone.

"Oh?"

"Remember all those notices Nicole has brought

home from school over the years warning us that 'Your child has been exposed to head lice'?"

"Yeah?"

"Well, guess what?"

"No. No, no, no," I whisper into the receiver. "Do *not* tell me this, Sam. Not now. Nikki can't have lice. I can't handle—I'll never be able to get through—"

"Listen, I don't want you to panic, but I think she's already spread them to Brianna and me."

Don't panic?! I want to shout back at her. *Do you have any idea what this is going to do to my life?* Years' worth of contamination concerns pale in comparison to the new images I'm already conjuring up. Bugs crawling everywhere. People screaming, B-movie style. I can't even begin to fathom all the havoc that I, and now my entire family, can wreak on the world.

Twenty minutes later, I rush into the house to find Samantha crouched over Nicole, a bright lamp propped just above their heads. Nikki's in tears. Brianna is also. Samantha looks frazzled.

"Well??"

"It's Mrs. Hansley's first-grade class," Sam says with her eyes still locked on a handful of hair she's holding up to the light. "A whole bunch of the kids have wound up with them."

"And you two?" I ask, afraid of the answer.

"I've already found a few nits in Brianna's hair, and, well, *I* am itching like crazy. I'm guessing Nicole brought the bugs home a few days ago and that we shared a brush after that."

"Damn it!" I bark, then demand that Sam drop what she's doing and come inspect *my* hair.

I check out clean. Sam jokes that the little critters are far more interested in the girls' shoulder-length hair than in my near crew-cut. An hour later, I beg her to check me again. I know she must have missed the lice colony taking up residence on my head.

It's getting late, but our night is just starting. Sam's been to the store for special lice shampoo and has treated both girls' heads. Now she's picking through their hair ten to twenty strands at a time, looking for lice eggs, or nits as they're called. The bugs themselves, she tells me, are generally too small and quick to be caught alive.

Sam takes a break and Nikki walks over to me. "I'm scared," she whispers, reaching her arms out my way for a hug.

"Everything's going to be fine," I say, backing up one step and then another. Nicole's a sharp six-year-old, but I can see in her eyes that she just can't process why Daddy won't put his arms around her. How could she? What kid—or adult, for that matter—could ever understand the paranoia that would keep me from being a father at a time like this, when I'm most needed as one?

At about midnight, Sam finishes going through both girls' hair. From what we've learned on the Internet tonight, we'll have to do this nightly for weeks.

We put the girls to bed, and Sam tells me I need to check her now. I insist that I can't. She says I have no choice. Finally I give in, but curse her under my breath with each nit I find. The plastic gloves and shower cap I'm wearing are hardly enough protection to quell my fears of becoming contaminated, and, worse yet, of becoming a launching pad for these bugs to attack everyone around me. "Lice can't jump and they certainly can't fly," Sam assures me. I don't believe her. What does she know about insects or, for that matter, about my uncanny ability to harm everyone around me?

When we finish for the night, I force myself outside. I don't want to talk to the stars tonight. I'm pissed at them for letting this happen. As I write on an index card a few minutes later, *This isn't fair. I'm not ready. I'm on the edge now. Very afraid.*

Samantha's in bed and suggests I come join her. I can't do that. Can't get that close. I roll out a sleeping bag on my den floor and rock myself to sleep.

When morning arrives, I fire off an e-mail to our entire staff at the station, explaining that my daughters have head lice. I almost always use my own headphones at work, but every now and then I'll put on a station pair, and I can't remember whether or not I did yesterday. I've already spent hours playing back my virtual tapes of the day. But as usual, they're of no help at all.

"Better to err on the safe side with a note," I explain to Samantha, when she asks what I'm doing.

"But you *don't have* lice," she snaps back at me, not understanding that this is an assumption my *what-if* thinking couldn't possibly accept. "If you don't have lice, you *can't* spread them to anyone else." Six hours worth of hair-checking last night has left Sam less than sympathetic to my OCD paranoia.

I show my compassion by waiting a full ten minutes before demanding another inspection of my hair.

Time is ticking away, and I'm in a panic over the David Brinkley introduction. I don't want to do it anymore, not when it will place him and so many others in imminent danger. I head into the station early and plead my case to our station manager. I tell him about the whole lice thing, how I've been up all night, how I feel like shit. It would really be better if Kitty did this alone, I insist. But he says it's too late, that everyone's expecting the two of us, together. I kick myself for not having invented a better excuse.

Before I know it, it's two o'clock and I'm in the VIP waiting area for Perspectives '97. Kitty is approaching now and my scalp is itching like crazy. I can feel all those little bugs Sam insists I don't have: they're jumping with excitement, waiting for the perfect opportunities to spring off my head. I want so badly to scratch my scalp, but I've made it more than an hour now without touching my hair. My hands are clean, or at least as clean as I could get them in the station bathroom just before I left. Hand-scrubbing strikes even me as a silly solution to head-lice concerns. But it's what I know, so it's what I do.

Soon Kitty and I are ushered into the luxury trailer serving as a green room for the symposium's keynote speakers. There, sitting right in front of me, is the host of ABC's *This Week with David Brinkley*. Introductions are made. We're told it will still be some time before we're needed on stage, to take a seat and make ourselves comfortable.

Help. What am I doing here? How selfish of me to even risk sharing my family's plague with an American icon!

Now I'm sitting just inches from this legend I've watched on TV for years, making small talk and shaking inside like an electric jackhammer. This should be a highlight of my career; I've worked hard to get to the place in this industry that would put me in the same room with a guy like David Brinkley. I should relish this moment. Instead I want to dash for the door.

The hands on the wall clock are moving in slow motion. I wish there was a way for me to confess, for the topic of lice to come up in conversation. Ever so coyly, I scope out Brinkley's thinning hair. Is there enough of it for the bugs to be interested? I hear Sam insisting that I don't have lice, that I can't give them to anybody if I don't have them myself.

Irrelevant, Doubt fires back. *Entirely irrelevant.*

The trailer door opens and in walks Brian Mulroney, the former prime minister of Canada. It seems he and Brinkley know one another and begin chatting. I do my best to disappear in my seat. Finally someone tells us it's time to go on, and in a fuzzy blur I follow Kitty to a lectern on a stage in front of an audience of thousands. This would be the part that might frighten most people. For me, it's a breath of fresh air. The sea of heads out there is a safe distance away. If I can just keep my nonexistent bugs off the microphone in front of me for the next two minutes, I know I'm home free.

Our voices give way to thunderous applause. Brinkley walks on. We exit. I beeline it for the bathroom and wash my hands.

October 31, 10:00 p.m. Whoa, baby, that
was close. I wanted to quit when I got
home tonight—not just slack off on the
Project for a little while, but formally quit.
I'm off the OCD scale. 10-plus.

A good five hours have now passed since the
Brinkley introduction, and still I am shaking with
fear as I write the words on the index card. It's
Halloween night, and the kid who interrupts my
journaling with his knock on our door reminds me
of the irony.

"Trick or treat."

Yeah, that's what my project is, one or the other.
Maybe it's the former and I'm wasting my time . . .

If I don't start writing on this card now, I
know I'm done, for good. Let me just put
this down in ink: I am NOT quitting.

Over the next two days, Samantha and I spend vir-
tually every waking minute at home going through
hair. At three hours per head check—except mine,
which takes roughly ten minutes to turn up nothing—we're finding it next to impossible to keep up
with the process.

Head lice, we've learned, are much more common than we'd thought. In fact, it seems every parent we know has either been through this ordeal before or, thanks to several outbreaks at our school, is going through it now. This is little consolation to me. As far as I'm concerned, we're a bunch of lepers.

My OCD paranoia is reaching new levels. I want to quarantine our family, to put a fumigation tent over our house and never leave it. That, of course, is not an option; so instead, I add to the girls' misery by doing everything I can to isolate them from the outside world. No friends. No trips to the store. No human contact.

Tensions mount sky-high at home as Sam struggles to hold things together. I all but move into my little den, eating and sleeping there and doing my best to hide from my wife and daughters, who are living in shower caps at my insistence. The plastic caps made me feel better for a while. But as always, Doubt found a way to intervene, prompting me to question whether lice might eat right through plastic or, for that matter, any other protective material we could think to use.

When I'm not obsessing about whom I might have contaminated with the bugs I don't have, I spend hours on the Internet researching lice and their treatment, a process Jackie would warn me is becoming an OCD ritual. I pore over online bulletin boards dealing with lice, hoping for answers to my *what-if* questions. Unfortunately, very few people are as imaginative as I am with their particular queries.

And still I promise myself I won't give up on my project. In between all the hair inspections and the research and the mental reviews and the pleas for reassurance, I force myself to fill up one index card after another with rambling notes, attempting at every step to capture all the OCD horror and make whatever sense of it I can relative to my new cardboard belief model that I carry with me everywhere. So much of what I wind up putting on the cards is downright depressing. Every once in a while, though, some illusory light bulb will turn on just above my head, and I'll find myself thinking, *Yeah, that's the ticket.* Such is the case tonight, just over seventy-two hours after all the nit-picking began. I grab an index card and scribble out what I decide is a whole new way of looking at this louse-y timing:

> *November 2, Day 13. Here I am cursing this lice infestation, when instead I should be thankful for the growth opportunities it presents . . . Are there not wonderful lessons right before me? Lice are like bad thoughts infesting my mind. It's not enough to remove those thoughts. I must also be vigilant of the "seeds" or "eggs" they plant; if not, they will go on to create additional problems.*

The treatment process is tedious, much
like my project. I cannot do it alone. I need
to take proactive measures. I need to re-
lease those elements not under my control.
Yes, clearly this challenge is a blessing,
a huge opportunity to grow.

It's nearly midnight again, and Sam is calling me to come get started on her hair. A blessing? Yeah, right.

■

Another week of hair-checking passes. Day after day I check out clean. Day after day my twisted OCD logic comes up with new ways in which I might contaminate everyone around me. I stop sitting in chairs for fear of transferring a stray nit-infested hair, and stop sending mail for fear of shipping off a bug looking to hitchhike. Doubt loves that one. That I might single-handedly bring down the entire U.S. Postal Service.

My den continues to be my safety shelter at home. In there, I can hide from Sam and the girls and their lethal ponytails. Unfortunately, the room offers little protection from my growing library of looped virtual videos, now showing just-out-of-focus recaps of my every encounter over the past two or three weeks.

Though I'm struggling to admit it, I find myself

increasingly distracted these days. Even our listeners are beginning to notice. "Tell Bell it's Wednesday," a caller barks after I go through an entire hour referring to the *Tuesday* edition of the Afternoon News. It kills me to think that perhaps my studio safe haven is now part of the war zone.

November 11, Day 22. Why is it that when I stand under these stars at night, gazing upward at the magnificent heavens, I seem to "get it" so clearly. And yet by the next morning, I'm right back in my house of horrors again . . .

The pattern is starting to take its toll on me. I am the prize fighter who keeps getting off the mat a second before he's called down for the count. Sam is worried again. Jackie would be too, if I'd let her know yesterday about the extent of my troubles. It was our first phone session, though, and I wanted to put the best face on things. Pretty stupid, I guess, paying a therapist to hear lies about my well-being.

Focus, I tell myself, as I turn back to my index card to wrap things up for the night. I write down the reminder Kenny Loggins is singing in my head:

Are you gonna wait for your sign, your miracle? Stand up and fight . . . This is it.

twenty-two

fast-forward 5 weeks

Passion—Life side of the pyramid, *Reverence* level. Passion is my word of the day, this chilly Saturday in December, and I whisper it to myself as Samantha pulls our minivan into the parking lot of our local Christmas tree farm.

Sam stops the van, and the girls gush out like water through a broken main. I stay behind a second or two, try to pump some courage into my veins. To believe in life, I remind myself, I've got to take part in it. And this is why I've come with the girls today—to be a part of our annual Christmas tree outing, one of the many Christian and Jewish holiday traditions that Sam and I have carried into our inter-faith family. Unfortunately, there are few things in the world that scare me more than using someone else's beat-up old saw with a loose and lethal blade, or strapping something as big and awkward as a six-foot Douglas fir to the top of our car.

"Come *oooonn,* Daddy!"

Brianna's high-pitched voice pierces the frosty air from halfway across the field. She and Nicole are running—sprinting, really—from one tree to another, thrilled, I'm sure, to be out without hats, now that our lice ordeal is behind us at long last.

Sam waves an arm at me, and I make my way over to her. Slung across her left shoulder is a curved rough-cut saw blade on a wooden stick about three feet long. Sure enough, the bolt that holds the two pieces together appears to be loose.

"I'm not touching that thing," I whisper curtly in her ear.

"I understand," Sam says between the gritted teeth of the big smile she's flashing at the girls, still off at a distance. "I think you've made that perfectly clear."

We walk on, both doing our best to stay focused on our children, the one thing that still bridges our disparate worlds.

"This one, Daddy," Nicole shouts all of sudden from about thirty feet away. She is bouncing up and down like a clown on a pogo stick.

"Watch where you're stepping!" I bark back at her. "You're going to trample next year's sprigs."

Undeterred, Nicole keeps up her Tigger-like springing. Sam heads over to have a look.

"Hey, not that one. *This* one," Brianna yells from a row or two over, swinging her arms just in front of a passing family of four.

"Damn it, Sam, will you *pleeeease* keep an eye on your youngest," I snarl. "She just about slammed into that kid."

Easy there, big guy, I remind myself. You can get through this. *Believe* you can. Show some *strength*. Show some *passion*. I turn my back on the three of them, do my best to regroup as the rest of my family decides to press on.

Ten minutes pass. Then ten minutes become twenty, and twenty become sixty. Still no tree. I'd have settled for the first one we saw, if it'd meant we could just get the hell out of here. But the girls can't reach a consensus to save their lives.

Finally, a chorus of voices shouts, "*This* one!"

"Whatever," I growl. "Let's just get things moving."

Nikki and Bri begin arguing over who gets to cut down the tree. Sam assures them they can each have a turn. I make a show of being fascinated with something elsewhere, so as to avoid the situation altogether. My head is aching and pounding and throbbing with doubt.

The girls each take a few minutes with the saw before deciding that the task is bigger than either of them. Samantha goes to work next and puts a good-sized notch in the trunk. But even from thirty feet away, I can hear her grunting as our stubborn tree holds its ground against the dull blade's attack.

"Daddy, *you* take a turn," Nicole hollers over to me.

"Oh, that's all right," I shout back. "You girls are having so much fun."

Clearly, Samantha is not. Her shirt is dark with sweat. She looks exhausted.

You're pathetic, I tell myself. *Go help your wife.* But I can't. Can't touch that old saw. I'll pay the price for years. I just know that I will.

"*Daaaa*dy," Nicole begs. She is now standing next to me and tugging on my sleeve. "Mommy needs help."

As she has so many times in the past, Samantha jumps to my rescue without missing a beat. "I've got it, girls. Don't you worry."

"But why can't Daddy help?" Bri asks, prompting Sam to look up from her saw.

"He just can't, sweetheart," my wife says, now panting and running the back of a hand across her forehead. "He just can't."

I turn away, ashamed, and drop my head. I count the minutes until the tree finally, mercifully, comes tumbling to the ground.

So now the jig is up. My charade is over. I am exposed forever for the freak that I am.

II PAUSE Exposed as a freak. This is how it always felt when I got caught falling prey to my OCD—at least at first. The stab of fear. The slap of shame. The crushing weight of utter despair. Everything ruined for all eternity.

But then, always, I would find a way to talk myself out of trouble one more time. Always. The night of the Christmas tree fiasco, I'd call the girls over and explain that Daddy wasn't feeling well today, or that my back was bothering me, or that I'm allergic to sawdust. Something. I'd come up with something. I always did. The girls would understand. They always did.

I became the master of deceit.

Still, there were growing signs that my magic act was wearing thin. Especially at work. Maybe I'd pulled one too many rabbits out of my hat, resorted to one too many elaborate sleights of hand. I don't know; perhaps it was all in my imagination. It just seemed there were ever more offhand comments and questions about my habits, ever more sideways glances and puzzled looks. Not from listeners; they hadn't a clue. It was the dozen or so people I worked with most directly who had me concerned. Like the security guard who couldn't understand why I chose to park in the spot farthest from the station (and easiest to get into and out of), even after he'd spelled out twice how I was complicating his rounds. Or our engineering staffers, who would scratch their faces in confusion when I'd point out the smallest, most ludicrous technical problems. "Am I missing something?" our chief engineer would ask me each time, his eyebrows always hoisted high.

A radio newsroom is a loud, charged, and intimate place. Phones, scanners, TV monitors, intercoms, news wires, network satellite feeds—all amid four walls positioned far too close to each other. One's best chance for privacy, I learned early on, is simply to blend in. Fortunately, the business is full of independent misfits with every imaginable oddity. Eccentrics everywhere. Clearly my own peculiarities were far more pronounced than most. Still, quirks are quirks. And *quirks* were what I always wrote off my most visible compulsions as. "Oh, just an old *quirk* of mine," I'd explain in response to all kinds of questions about my many odd habits.

The Quirk Defense had worked well for me over the years, especially in defending my need to roll tape on my every hour of airtime. "It's not as if I listen back to these things," I'd always huff with feigned indignation, intimating that the whole practice was more of a superstitious thing, really, like a quirky basketball player who's got to pull his socks up and down twice before heading out on the floor. The thing was, though, I *did* listen back. And they knew it. They would see me with my headphones on after the show, hunching over a tape recorder, hitting the Rewind button again and again. Some of them, I'm guessing, even knew what I was up to.

It was just so complicated in those days, with Doubt always suggesting that I was screwing our clients. *Are you really certain you played that commercial spot that you just signed off on?*

How could I not be certain? The process was so simple and unambiguous. I'd follow a computer-generated commercial log that told me precisely when and where to play each recorded spot. Sears airs at 12:17, Big O Tires a minute after that. Each spot was self-contained on a cartridge that looked like an old eight-track tape, and each was labeled with a unique tracking number that matched up with my log. All I had to do was plug the cartridge into a special playback machine, hit the Start button, and check off that the commercial aired.

My problem, though, was that I couldn't seem to trust my own bookkeeping. The Sears spot would end, and I'd put my check mark through the word Sears on my program log. But then Doubt would start messing with me. *Do you* really *remember playing the commercial?* The Sears jingle could still be fresh in my head. The playback machine could still be flashing its "spot completed" light, and still there I'd be second-guessing myself.

"Hey, Kitty," I'd resort to saying. "I must be going nuts. Did we just air that Sears ad a minute ago?"

"The Sears ad?" my partner would ask, eyes narrowed and focused on mine. "It *just* ended, you big goober!"

"Right," I'd apologize, shaking my head. "Of course. Thanks."

Crisis solved.

But Kitty wasn't paying attention. Can you really trust her? Doubt would remind me it was a good thing I was rolling tape on the show—tape I'd play back for myself just as soon as the show ended at seven o'clock. I'd hear the Sears jingle and think everything was fine. But then I'd start questioning whether I'd gotten my jingle tunes right. *Was that Sears or Home Depot?* Better play back the entire spot. One more time to make sure the announcer actually said Sears.

Play. Rewind. Play. Rewind. I couldn't stop myself.

On a good night, it was just Sears or some other individual spot that required my checking. On a bad one though, Doubt could convince me to play back my entire three-hour show, checking each and every spot against the commercial log in front of me. Like everything else with my twisted

OCD logic, I'd convince myself that I was doing the right thing by being so meticulous; after all, I owed it to our clients. God Almighty, did they ever have a friend in me, as did our general management. Could my bosses have asked for a more conscientious employee?

Night after night I played back my airchecks. Never—not even once—did I find a checked-off spot that I'd failed to air.

▶ PLAY "Hey, Jeff, catch!"

It takes my brain a good second or two to figure out it's a set of car keys that is headed my way.

"How 'bout *you* drive us home?" says my boss, Ken, more as a statement than a question, really. "After that glass of wine at lunch, I'm thinking I'd just as soon not be behind the wheel."

It's late December, and we've just wrapped up our staff Christmas party at a downtown restaurant. Our news director, Paul, and I are walking with Ken to his nearby car. Never for a second have I considered the possibility that I'll be asked to drive us back to the station.

"I, uh, I'd . . . rather not," I blurt out, searching in a panic for some reasonable explanation. I haven't had any wine and they know it, so that excuse is out of the question. Just seconds ago, I was goofing around with the gang, so I can't tell them I'm feeling sick either. The truth? Yeah, right.

Paul picks up on my hesitation. "Here, give me the keys," he says, reaching out his hand. We all walk a few steps in awkward silence.

I've got to say something. *Something.* Here, my boss has asked a simple favor of me—for the most noble of reasons, no less—and what have I done? Dismissed him outright. Not good.

Ken and Paul strike up a conversation. I let myself slip a step or two behind. *Say something, damn it. Anything.*

"I have a confession to make," I finally mutter.

Ken and Paul stop, await my next words. I myself have no idea what they might be.

"I'm . . . I'm kinda phobic about driving other people's cars."

"Really?" they both say, almost a little too much in unison, as if scripted that way.

"Yeah, it's this hang-up I've always had."

Good one, Jeff, I reassure myself. That should end that. But instead it somehow spawns a flood of questions.

"No kidding," Paul says. "Anyone's car?"

"Would it matter if the owner wasn't in the car with you?" Ken wants to know.

Paul: "Rental cars too?"

Ken: "Has it always been a problem for you?"

Now my head is overheating, the way it does

when the circuitry up there feels like it's about to fry.

"Well, actually, I'm not too big on driving with passengers, in general," I tell them before thinking through where that answer might lead.

"Wow," Paul says. "So your wife must do all the driving?"

"Uh, yeah," I admit with some hesitation, imagining myself shrinking another foot or two with each step I take.

"Fascinating," Ken says, now shaking his head.

Soon we are getting into Ken's car. I am so lightheaded I could easily pass out. I console myself that the worst is over, only to find out that in fact it is not.

"I know this lady who has an extreme fear of cars," Ken volunteers, then proceeds to tell her story. I nod my head every now and then, do my best to sound interested. *God, I'm a freak,* I keep thinking to myself. *And a liar. And a fraud. And a horrible person. My life is over, and I deserve it to be.*

And then a few minutes later, my troubles compound. There, on the car ceiling just above my head, is a good-sized scratch in the fabric. *I must have put that there while climbing into the backseat,* I decide. *Now what to do?* I know I'm falling into the classic OCD trap of "transference," taking all my anxiety from one episode and moving it to another.

An eternity later, we pull into the station lot.

Ken and Paul get out of the car. I can't. I am glued to my seat.

"What's the problem?" Ken asks when he sees me staring at the ceiling.

"I, uh, think I may have put a scratch in your—"

"It's fine," Ken interrupts, using a tone a father might take with his four-year-old son. He is shaking his head, staring at me. "Come on now. Let's go."

I know two things in this instant that churn my stomach like spoiled milk: first, that I'm not as clever as I think I am; and second, that "quirky" will no longer suffice as an explanation for my quirks.

twenty-three

fast-forward 2 days

I guess I'd forgotten just how invigorating a stiff summer breeze can feel as it whistles past your ears, how refreshing a splash of salt water can taste at the corners of your mouth, how soothing a chorus of low-flying seagulls can sound at the end of a long afternoon on the Bay.

Slowly, though, it's all coming back to me now as the sun sinks with abandon toward the mighty Pacific. Dad and I are exhausted too, but in the best kind of way. After hours of short-tacking back and forth along the San Francisco shoreline and clear on through the Golden Gate, we are at long last enjoying the fruits of our labor: a spectacular, spinnaker-flying broad reach back to Alameda, where Samantha and Mom and a hearty steak dinner are awaiting us at a window table for four at The Rusty Scupper.

These past five hours have been pure nautical bliss. Even more importantly, they've afforded my father and me what we've most needed for at least a decade: some quality time together aboard The Boat—time to sail, talk, take in all the elements, give ourselves a fresh start at this whole boating thing. A father and son sharing a common bond and a common passion.

This is how I always dreamed it could be. This is how I always knew it was supposed to be.

Somewhere along the windward shoreline of Treasure Island, the sound of fluttering nylon snaps me out of my wind-and-sea trance. We are, I now realize, sailing directly into the mammoth shadow of the San Francisco–Oakland Bay Bridge, where sudden wind shifts are both frequent and unpredictable. The Boat's huge red, white, and blue spinnaker is folding itself in half in a loud and colorful demand for attention. A quick adjustment—to the spinnaker pole, the sheets, or most likely, to both—is clearly needed. I jump into action without even thinking.

"Got it," I shout to Dad on my way to the bow, pulling the slack out of the leeward sheet. I scurry forward, but I can't get there soon enough.

BAM!

Our confused aluminum spinnaker pole slams against the mast rigging. The massive parachute-like sail to which it's attached deflates itself before I can stop it.

"Come ON, God-damn-it!" I hear Dad yell from the cockpit. He is shaking his head back and forth in short and quick strokes, much as he always did in my youth when he wanted to make clear his disappointment with me.

Suddenly, a strong westerly crosses our stern and breathes new life into the flagging spinnaker. In an instant, the crisis is over. A smile returns to my father's face every bit as quickly. "Come on back," he says almost playfully, as if nothing ever happened.

But it's too late. The damage is done. Something deep inside of me has snapped that can't be put back together again. Mechanically, I about-face on the deck and return to the cockpit.

Now Dad and I are standing just inches apart. I am the ten-year-old kid who scrambled but failed to set the anchor just right in the river. I am the fifth-grader who tried to hang the fenders properly but still managed to put a scratch in The Boat's shiny fiberglass hull. I am the grown man with OCD staring into the eyes of his father.

With the fury of three decades worth of pent-up ire and resentment, I reach over and grip my hands to his shoulders.

"Don't you GET it?!" I shout into his face. "Can't you see what you've done to me?"

Dad is shaking now. There is fear in his eyes—fear and confusion—as I continue my tirade.

"YOU did this to me. Don't you get that. For the love of God, why can't you see it? Why can't you . . ."

BZZZZZZZZZZZZZ . . . A foghorn on the Bay Bridge cuts short my barrage of acid-filled words.

But it's not a foghorn. No. It's a higher-pitched sound, a jarring, strangely familiar sound.

My alarm. It's my alarm clock.

This is my bed. It's morning, and I'm in my bed. I have been dreaming. Dreaming the Dream again. The one I've been fighting with at least once a week for a good many months. The one that always leaves my skin clammy and my gut tied up in knots. I hate this damn dream and all its twisted variations. There are so many. Sometimes Dad and I are sailing on The Boat as we were tonight. Sometimes we're working on a project together, attempting to build or fix something or another. Sometimes we're just out taking a walk. Always, though, the dream sequence ends the same way—with me letting loose on my old man for all that he's done to screw me up royally.

Why do I keep doing this—blaming Dad in my dreams, night after night? I don't *really* hold him responsible, do I? I've seen the research. Genetics, not upbringing, almost certainly gave me my curse. Yeah, my quick-tempered father was capable of being a first-class prick, but then so too am I with Nicole and Brianna. And they seem to be fine. At worst, Dad and his militant perfectionism made me a checker—as opposed to a repeater or a hoarder or some other flavor of freak. Is that really so bad?

Isn't my bitter subconscious-self being a little tough on the poor guy?

Besides, I'm the one who carried the whole sick dependency thing right out of my youth and clear into adulthood. Me, not Dad. Is it really *his* fault that I'm still so hell-bent on checking with him on every major decision I make, so committed to securing his reassurance like a necessary stamp on an entrance visa, so determined to keep him from shaking his head in disappointment with me?

Compassion—*Others* side of my belief pyramid, *Resolve* level. I have got to find some compassion for my father, if only during my waking hours.

I get my opportunity on December 27, Project Day 68, as I note on my index cards. Our extended family is gathered at Mandi's place to celebrate Hanukkah, and Dad and I are in the backyard, catching up on things since our last visit together. We talk current events, as we always do. We talk computers and Internet sites and high-tech gadgets and other marvels of modern technology. And finally, inevitably, we wind up talking about the cata-strophic consequences of other people's screw-ups. This is what my father does for a living these days—speaks as an expert witness in insurance cases about what some poor schmo has done wrong in some deal. Since the two of us have already covered the news of the day and my coverage of it, I suppose it's only fair that I show at least some interest in Dad's latest courtroom testimony. Unfortunately, though, his who's-screwed-over-whom stories are always so OCD-charged for me. Always. The same old negli-gence triggers waiting for me again and again. I can't help wondering if he has any idea how badly he always sets me off, talking about some negligent driver or unqualified contractor.

For God's sake, doesn't he get it?

This is not my dream, though. I am not tempted to grab my father's shoulders and launch into my diatribe. I know, in reality, that Dad simply *doesn't* get it. It's not his fault. Normal people couldn't pos-sibly understand the nuances of my beast. I remind myself of this, and *Compassion*'s place on my believ-ing pyramid, as I put my game face on and attempt to jump into my father's one-sided conversation, even challenging myself to ask a few follow-up questions.

Mandi's holler of "Lunch!" a few minutes later saves me from at least a half-dozen OCD traps Dad and Doubt are conspiring to set. I am safe at the table, a handful of kids sandwiched between my father and me. But Dad pulls me aside as Mandi and Sam are clearing the last of the dishes.

"Can we tuck away for a minute?" he whispers.

"Sure," I say, trying but failing to read his face. I point toward the stairwell that leads up to Mandi's second-story den. We climb the stairs together in silence.

"Listen," Dad says when we get to the top, "I've been wanting to talk to you for a while about your OCD."

"O-*kaaaaaay*," I say, probably injecting far too much hesitation into that second syllable; I'm just not sure where he's planning to take things. In the three-plus years since I first told my family about my OCD, the subject has come up maybe twice in conversations with my father, both times at *my* introduction. Mom likes to tell me—over and over, in fact—that Dad's always asking her about how I'm doing, that he's very concerned about me, but that he's convinced I'll broach the topic with him when, and only when, *I* have something I'd really like to share. So this is a first.

"I, uh, I've been thinking a lot lately. . ." he says, stopping as if to weigh his options for the rest of this sentence. "Thinking about the role I must have played in bringing about your OCD."

My father's words hang uncomfortably in the air between us. He has put them out here, it strikes me, more as a statement than an apology really. A pronouncement. A declaration. A simple matter of fact that I'm free to do with as I see fit. Still, I can't help picking up on a certain sorrow in Dad's eyes, a vulnerability that I've never before noticed in them.

An awkward silence fills the room like smoke.

I'm supposed to say something, I suppose. But I can't. I'm speechless. I am still trying to make head or tail of what I've just heard. This is somehow another dream, albeit a daytime one with a much happier ending.

"I . . . I was pretty tough on you kids growing up," Dad continues, the corners of his mouth now slightly turned down.

Another long pause.

I've really got to say something. Anything. So I offer up the first words I can string together in my open-jawed mouth. "Oh, I dunno. You always tried—"

"No, I was tough on you and your sister," Dad interrupts. "And I'm still always trying to impose my own standards on the two of you. Take that new computer of yours."

"The e-Machine?"

"Yeah.

"You were so excited when you called to tell me about it. And what did I do? Point out all the things that I thought were missing."

"You've got high standards," I say. "You're a true perfectionist."

"Well, that's fine for my life, but I was so impatient with you and Mandi as kids, and now, with all that's happened with you, I can't help wondering—"

"You *were* impatient," I concede, surprising myself with my controlled, emotion-free candor. This whole conversation is so different from the one I've played out countless times in my recurring dream. "Truth be told, you were a pretty lousy father at times. But you *didn't* cause my OCD; some mutant gene in my body did. You've read enough of the research to know that, Dad."

Dad shakes his head, starts to say something.

"I can't tell you how much I appreciate the fact that we're just having this chat," I interrupt. "I hope you know how much this means to me, being able to put this kind of stuff on the table." My father and I have never talked openly about anything even remotely having to do with emotions. We have never said the words "I love you" to one another. And with a very few exceptions, we have never even shared a hug.

I decide to do something about the latter right now, and I put my arms around Dad. Our embrace has the awkwardness of two macho football players who, with great embarrassment, catch themselves getting carried away after a big play.

But it's a start. And it feels damn good for the five or ten seconds it lasts. And although I can't know it here, I will never again—not even once—dream the Dream again.

■

Exactly two weeks later I am standing at the kitchen counter with a phone receiver in my shaking left hand. *Pick up, Dad. Come on, damn it, pick up the friggin' phone.*

I have spent the past two hours filling and prepping our brand new hot tub, the one Samantha surprised me with for Christmas this year. It's all but ready for my inaugural dip. But after having watched the electrician install the wiring this morning, I've managed to convince myself that we did the hot tub installation all wrong at the first house we owned. Doubt has come up with a half-dozen electrocution *what-ifs* for me to ponder forever.

I want to call the new owners of that house and warn them of their impending perils, tell them to stay away from the damn thing or they'll surely die. But I know I can't; Jackie's all over me these days about disrupting other people's lives with my compulsive confessions. And that's why I'm calling Dad. He'd helped me with that whole decking project. He'll have some thoughts. I know I'll feel better if he'll just pick up the phone, if I can just run through every-thing with him.

"Hello." My father's voice is at the other end of the line.

Damn him for being there when I can't stop my-self from checking with him. Damn him for picking up the phone—doesn't he know it could be his pa-thetic son calling for another OCD fix?

Doesn't he get it?!

twenty-four

PAUSE

I need to share with you a few thoughts about windsurfing, and the powerful lesson the sport has taught me about living life in general, and battling OCD in particular. It's a lesson I learned, literally, back in the mid-1980s, when my every spare moment was spent on sailboarding adventures. I learned it metaphorically ten years later, when I found myself pining for the normalcy of those windsurfing years.

So simple, really: Sometimes, to move forward, you've got to fall back and trust.

I mean, there you are standing on your board on a windy day, lifting the mast-and-sail rig out of the water, and the only way to harness the wind is to lean back with the rig and all your weight—often until your head is just inches above the water—and wait that split second for a steady breeze to fill your sail and launch you ahead.

Such is a windsurfer's leap of faith. And such, I came to learn in early 1998, is the requisite process for getting a handle on OCD.

I had spent much of January and February "leaning back" and throwing my full weight into maneuvers that demanded of me every ounce of my trust. First there was the annual Yosemite trip with our extended family, during which I forced myself to avoid asking Samantha a single OCD question for three interminable days, all the while fending off one of Doubt's most vicious attacks in years. Then, a few days later, there was the half-hour KFBK tour I gave Nicole's entire first-grade class, all of them banging into each other and our equipment at every step of the way. And *then* a couple weeks after that: the Comstock Club luncheon, where I broke my cardinal no-contact-while-eating rule when actor/director Rob Reiner handed me his wallet with pictures as we discussed our kids over lunch.

Lean back. Trust. Wait for the wind.

Splat!

And that's the thing. Like the windsurfing novice who hasn't yet mastered the falling-back technique, I kept coming up short, and very wet, again and again. Instead of launching myself forward, I wound up flat on my back. Instead of feeling empowered by my success in fighting off checking compulsions in Yosemite, I let Doubt play catch-up with me from the moment I got home, hounding poor Sam for days, worse than ever. Instead of riding the momentum of my station tour for the kids, I got myself so worked up toward the end that Nicole's teacher later asked Sam if I was okay—*He just seemed so nervous.* And instead of relishing my luncheon chat with Rob Reiner, I let myself get caught in three OCD episodes before even leaving the parking lot afterward.

Splat. Splat. Splat.

Fortunately, as any sailboarder can attest to, at some point along the learning curve, you *do* begin getting the knack of harnessing the wind. You learn to control your faith-based fallback, to let this powerful unseen force scoop you up from the brink of impact and rocket you ahead at breakneck speed. You succeed at this sporadically at first, still spending a great deal of time in and just beneath the water. But then the whole process becomes second nature. Before you know it, you find yourself so caught up in the ride that you almost forget what it took to get you going on it.

That, I suppose, is where I was with things in

mid-February, 100-plus days into my project. Sailing along and not even noticing. And perhaps that's why I was so flabbergasted one night when I sat down to complete my "episodes card" for the day and came to appreciate the significance of what I'd just put down onto paper:

> Driving episodes: none

> Judgment episodes: none

> Safety episodes: none

> On-air episodes: none

> Germ episodes: none

> Envelope episodes: none

No OCD episodes the entire day. Nada. Zippo. Not a single one. This was a first for me, and it floored me to think that I never even realized it until that very moment.

I did have an episode to log the following night—in fact, three of them. And in the days after that, there were at least a half dozen I needed to record on my cards. A full week passed quickly, though, and at the end of it, I couldn't help noting not one, but two, major milestones:

February 21. Today I am four months into my project. One third of the way there. And at long last, I can honestly say that I am making progress, even if it's so much less than I would like it to be. Today also marks another first: one week of sustained progress. For seven days now, I have topped these cards on a positive note. I have been disciplining myself like never before and the payoff is clear. This whole believing model works, if only I will let it.

Seven days of triumphs. Seven days of genuine sustained progress. Seven days of feeling strong. Unbelievable. I'd had "good days" here and there over the past many years, but never in my recent memory had I managed to string together a full week of them. This was really something. At long last, my project was really sailing along.

And therein lay my greatest fear, one that again had me thinking back on all my windsurfing years. I just couldn't help remembering what would always happen when I'd get "in the groove" (as we'd say in those days), planing along at breakneck speed. I'd find myself getting scared every time. *You're riding above your skill level now; you know you can't sustain this*, some early ancestor of Doubt would always whisper. *Any minute now, you're going to crash and burn.*

And inevitably I would.

Here in late February, I was on an entirely different kind of thrill ride. But the growing insecurity and fear were eerily reminiscent of my windsurfing days. The fall was about to come. I knew this in my bones, and the marrow never lies.

The fall *did* come, all right. And right on cue.

It came when I was soaring along. When I was at the peak of my game, feeling the exhilaration of having finally harnessed the forces of nature—all the powers of a friendly universe, right there for the asking but available only to the true believers of this world who, against all odds, have learned how to tap it.

It came on a Thursday morning in early March.

PLAY I am soaking in our backyard hot tub, basking in the spring sunshine and in the glory of all my recent success. I am feeling downright cocky for the first time in years, mulling over the last month or so in my head, taking inventory of how far I've come and how much I've managed to accomplish. What a ride, I can't help thinking.

Psssst. Ever sort out that whole conversation you had with Dad a while back about firewalls?

Doubt is whispering to me. It loves the Dad topic, knows it's always so charged with anxiety and fear.

Warning lights and sirens go off in my head. I close my eyes and try to ignore Doubt, try to think instead about anything and everything else. But it's Dad's face I see. Dad's voice I hear. Before I can stop myself, I cue up a tape of that last conversation with him. We are talking about phone lines. I am asking Dad what he thinks would be involved in running an extra line to my den. I can hear him telling me that, well, that could be tough, since it might require we find a way to get around a firewall.

I pause the tape.

Have I ever negligently drilled through any fire-walls in the past?

Frantically I begin reviewing every hole I have ever bored in every wall of every house I have ever owned or rented. I come up empty. Nothing. Not a single trouble scenario recorded on any of my tapes.

The TV cable line in San Bruno. Have a look at that one, Doubt suggests.

The TV cable line in San Bruno. Yeah, I re-member that cable. I ran it between the basement and the living room of the house we were renting. There were no firewalls involved. I'm certain of that. Still, I dig out my tape of the installation just to be sure. The image is predictably fuzzy, but I can see myself drilling through something. It's not a fire-wall, but it is something wooden. A heating duct. That's what it is. An old-fashioned heating duct made out of plywood.

Shit!

But wait a minute. Didn't I seal up that hole? With a special gasket and caulking, in fact? I'm cer-tain that I did. I try to fast-forward to that part of my installation memory. I can't find it, though; the tape is blurry. I reassure myself next that I'd gotten permission from the landlord beforehand, and had actually shown him after the fact how the line was run. Unfortunately, both of those scenes, too, are all but static on my virtual tapes.

Refocus, Jeff, I tell myself. Think about the believing pyramid. Think about *Release. Self* side, *Surrender* level. Release this whole thing. Do it now.

But I can't.

The heat of the hot tub becomes unbearable. I know I've got to get out of here, go run and hide. But I can't even move, I'm so paralyzed with fear.

This is the Fall, the one I've seen coming for weeks. No way to stop it now, not even a chance. At any second—this very one or the next—I'll begin cart-wheeling head over heels at twenty miles per hour, paying the price for this exhilarating ride, as I've done so many times before on rivers and lakes. The only difference here is that this time I am already in the water. This time the rest of the world is closing in on me for the crash.

■

I call Sam at work and start firing off all the *what-if's* Doubt is feeding me: *What if the duct was, in fact, part of the whole firewall system? What if the cable itself is a fire hazard because of passing hot air? What if you didn't properly seal your hole in the duct, and some deadly gases from the basement get into the heating system and hence the house?*

Sam tells me everything is just fine. She is sure of that. But what does she know? I need an expert. Someone with a solid understanding of heating systems. Someone with an engineering degree. Someone with an insurance broker's appreciation of fire hazards. Someone like . . . Dad. The problem is he is off on one of his sailing adventures, bobbing around somewhere in the middle of nowhere, gone for at least another three weeks. I know I can and will check with my father just as soon as he gets back, but in the meantime, I need a reassurance fix from somebody. So I corner my brother-in-law at a get-together a few days later.

Poor Uncle Mikey, as we all call my sister's husband, Mike. A mechanic by trade, he's one of the handiest, most mechanical guys I know—and because of that, he, like my father, is a prime resource for my checking. The difference is, Uncle Mikey is onto me. The two of us are like brothers, and have been for years. He knows all too well from our many conversations what a vicious cycle reassurance creates. So when I share with him my concerns, he narrows his eyes.

"You know we shouldn't go there," he says.

"But this one's different," I explain. "I *really* need to know. I'm hurting bad."

Now what's the poor guy supposed to do? He gives in. I win. Especially when he shakes his head and laughs, as he tells me how ludicrous my thinking on all this is.

Now I feel better.

But only for an hour or two. Our conversation is not enough to stop my tapes. So I read up on heating systems. I hold an old scrap of coaxial cable above a heating vent to see how hot it gets. I come up with all kinds of clever experiments.

Still, I can't stop myself from playing back my fuzzy images of the installation and my conversation with our landlord.

In a rare moment of clear thinking, I realize I need to talk to Jackie. I make arrangements for a special phone session, and at the appointed hour we begin tackling another exposure together. Step by excruciating step, Jackie leads me through the worst of my fears surrounding the whole cable issue. For a full forty minutes I imagine out loud every hypothetical disaster that Doubt can come up with. Nothing is too far-fetched for this little exercise, and with Jackie's coaxing, I blab on and on about God-awful catastrophes, all the while watching my anxiety and heart rate climb off the charts.

And then something happens. I suddenly get very tired of hearing myself talk. I become almost bored with the entire process. Somehow, it's as if I've managed to wring out every last drop of anxiety from each of the once highly charged words I've been using to describe my very worst nightmares. "Fire," "flames," "suffocation," and so many other of Doubt's vocabulary favorites could now just as easily be flavors of ice cream; they have lost all their emotional meaning to me.

"Great, Jeff!" Jackie exclaims when I concede this to her. "That's the *flooding* effect we're looking for. Outstanding."

I've made a good decision, calling Jackie for this exercise. I know this was a good *investment*, in the lexicon of my believing pyramid. I can almost feel some unseen force stopping my fall, if only temporarily. But I have a new problem, one that becomes more clear to me with each passing hour: My physical anxiety—the tightness in my chest, the knot in my gut, the incessant pressure behind my eyes—it's still all right there, right where it was before Jackie's exposure. The only difference now is that it doesn't seem to be "attached" to the cable obsession anymore. It's just *there,* trapped in my body.

I once read that free-floating anxiety is the most intolerable sensation a human being can experience, and that OCD might, in fact, be a defense mechanism of sorts designed to confront it. The theory goes that OCs "assign" their biochemical anxiety to particular fears (obsessions) so that they can then take ritualistic actions (compulsions) to feel as if they're at least doing something constructive.

I don't know about all that, but I do know I keep catching myself working backwards from my tied-up gut, trying to make sense of all my cable anxiety and transferring the whole bundle of it to whatever triggers just happen to come up. A tire tread. A lane change. A passing ambulance. A handshake with a guy at work who's still recovering from surgery. Trigger by trigger, I keep my bundle of anxiety alive and always attached to *something*, passing it ever forward, like a baton in a marathon relay race. The process becomes exhausting and takes a huge toll on my ability to focus. Kitty and I host an awards program, and I fumble my way through my lines, obsessing over my sneeze earlier in the night and Doubt's insistence that I got everyone sick.

I am exhausted. Bitter. Aching inside and out. And I am falling ever downward, arms and legs flailing like some poor stiff in an action flick who's just been sent flying with a punch through a penthouse window.

March 22. This project and life are slipping away from me. I have lost my balance and fallen, and now I can't seem to get back on

my feet. OCD's twin pillars of fear and
doubt are square in my path and seem-
ingly immovable. Again I find myself on
the verge of quitting, wanting desperately
to roll over, defeated on my path, and let
life trample me as it might.

Is this even constructive, putting such wretched thoughts down on index cards, day after day? What's the point? Clearly my project is going nowhere, and quickly.

■

March 25. Day 156. I am curled up under my sheets in our empty house after having called in sick an hour ago. I can't be at work today. I can't even fathom getting myself out of this bed. My fear, my anxiety, my paranoia—all have reached levels that frighten me in ways I can't even begin to understand. I feel more empty inside than ever before. Everything around me is dark and fuzzy around the edges. Clearly, this is the worst bout of depression I've ever had to deal with, and Samantha is fed up with my stubborn insistence on relying solely on my project to get myself through it. Jackie too is suggesting that my current approach, even with her supplemental coaching and treatment, is hardly working. The two of them, my wife and my therapist, keep bringing up meds. I myself am so hopelessly lost that I'm questioning everything: all my core beliefs, all my believing words on my ridiculous pyramid, and all my collective hours of quiet time under the stars.

Who am I fooling?

Day 156. As I put down tonight on a journal index card—one I'm fairly certain will be the last I ever waste my time on—I can only pray this particular day will someday prove to be "the bottom."

I can only pray this day will somehow mark the end of the Fall.

twenty-five

fast-forward 9 days

Carole Johnson knows all too well about days like my Day 156. She tells me this over sandwiches and fries a week and a half later, on Day 165. This is the lunch I've been putting off for the past five months. Why, I'm not certain. I thought maybe I was ready to talk with another obsessive-compulsive today. But now, sitting here across from one, I'm not so sure. Maybe I'm still not up to seeing my reflection in somebody else.

Carole explains to me that she's a *repeater*, another common OCD creation I've never really understood. She says her obsessions almost always involve random catastrophic thoughts, like *something really bad is going to happen to so-and-so,* and the only way for her to "clear" these thoughts is to carry out specific patterns, generally involving sets of three. She might, for instance, be setting the table for dinner one night when the thought crosses her mind that a loved one is going to get hurt or die. In order to save herself the agony of obsessing about this horrific notion for hours, she performs a simple thought-clearing ritual, putting the plate that's in her hand on the table, and removing and replacing it precisely three times.

For whatever strange reasons, *three* is Carole's magic number, and its power over her is enormous. Sometimes it's a toilet needing three flushes, or a light switch requiring three on-and-off cycles. Once, Carole tells me, she had one of her "intrusive thoughts" while going through a hotel doorway hundreds of miles from home. Circumstances kept her from making more than two passes back through the doorway right then, and she had to leave without completing her ritual. For more than a decade Carole obsessed about that particular thought. Nothing could save her from its grip until a return trip to that hotel finally provided an opportunity for exactly one more pass through the exact same doorway.

"Can you *believe* that, Jeff?" Carole asks.

I can, which is strange considering I have never felt compelled to repeat any action in sets of three, or for that matter, in sets of any other size. *My* responses to obsessions are so much more logical than those of repeaters. At least that's what I always try to tell Jackie and Sam, both of whom generally raise an eyebrow and all but laugh in my face before I can finish. Still, I can't deny that the *power* of my compulsions is every bit as strong as what I'm hearing today.

Carole's stories scare me, not because they're so hard to believe, but because they're so familiar. We are, when it comes right down to it, no different at all. Nothing more than opposite sides of the same coin—one that some cruel twist of fate has sent spinning on its edge, out of control and nearly out of circulation.

It takes me a good twenty minutes to get past my hang-ups with talking to Carole, but then before I know it, I find myself sharing much more than I mean to. She is just such a comfortable audience, one of those rare people who can make you feel so at ease that you don't even realize you're blabbing on until it's all out there and way too late to take any of it back.

We talk about my depression, and my checking patterns, and my years' worth of wasted time and money before I found Jackie. We talk about our shared belief in a "greater good" and free will and the power of positive thinking. And at some point, the conversation comes around to my journaling project.

"You know those index cards you're filling up aren't just for you," Carole says.

"I'm sorry . . .?"

"Your index card notes about OCD and doubt—" She is leaning across the table now, staring into my eyes. "A lot of people are going to find themselves in those notes."

Now I know that I've said too much. This is my secret. My unspoken, deep desire to do something constructive with all my index cards. To keep my bargain with the stars and share my story for a greater good. Like Jampolsky's cancer support-group kids. Or my old AA friends. I want to do this too, if for no other reason than the selfish one of giving meaning to all the lost years.

But this isn't something I talk about out loud. Not even with Sam. Besides, the whole notion is pretty laughable right now. What a frightful, depressing anthology of failures any book of mine would be.

Carole must read my face. She reaches across the table and puts my hands in hers, much like a grandmother might. "It will all make sense some day, Jeff," she says. "Mark my words, it will all make sense."

I leave our lunch shaking my head. In just

over one hour, Carole Johnson has managed to do what neither Samantha nor Jackie nor any of my self-help books has been able to accomplish in weeks: somehow snap me out of my funk. Maybe it was the talk about the index cards, or our discussion about free will. Maybe it was just being in the company of another obsessive-compulsive. All I know is that the dark and fuzzy edges are gone from my field of view. I am back on my sailboard, again harnessing the wind.

Day 156 is behind me now. It *will* go down as the low point of my entire project. Of this, I am as positive as an OC can be.

There are certain things you come to accept living with severe OCD—like the need to set realistic limits on your recovery expectations. Checkers with driving issues, for example, will probably never find themselves behind the wheel of a taxi or a Greyhound bus. I'm sure some therapists would beg to differ, but it strikes me that such acceptance is hardly a cop-out. I'd go so far as to call it healthy. The problem, of course, is the very fine line between acceptance and avoidance.

I am walking this line often in the early spring of '98, and I know I'm guilty of winding up on the wrong side of it more often than I should. Still, there *are* at least a few items that I'm certain will always be on my "necessary acceptance" list, and chief among these is my inability to chaperone the girls, without Sam's help, in a room full of kids falling all over each other. It's just not going to happen. Samantha will always have to be the one to take them to Chuck E. Cheese and supervise their afternoons at the playground and gym. I struggle enough just watching our girls play soccer, bumping into their teammates and stepping all over everyone and everything along the sidelines. I can't even fathom taking part in their scouting meetings and troop-wide get-togethers. And after the Christmas tree debacle, I certainly can't risk getting caught again.

Samantha understands all this. She accepts my regular absences from so many aspects of the girls' day-to-day lives. She has grown accustomed to having to cover for me. So a few weeks back when Nicole's Brownie troop announced a father-daughter dance—scheduled for tonight—Sam was hardly surprised to hear me say I couldn't possibly go. "I assumed as much," she said, "It's okay. I told Nikki you wouldn't be available."

I hate the idea of being *unavailable* for my daughter's first dance, but, let's be real, I don't have a choice—or so I'm convinced until several hours after my lunch with Carole, when I'm driving home feeling especially bold, if not downright invincible.

"Nicole, you and I need to get ourselves

dressed," I announce as I throw open the front door to our house.

"For what?" she asks, looking over at her mother who is every bit as confused.

"The dance."

My answer could have been "Disneyland" or "a ride to the moon" and still not have elicited the giddy excitement I can see in my seven-year-old's eyes. Nicole scrambles off to her room to get dressed. Samantha pulls me into the den.

"What's all this about?" she wants to know, almost as if looking for some catch or ulterior motive.

"Just feeling kind of brave tonight," I say, knowing what a false bravado mine is. I've already accepted that Doubt is going to make me pay for all this in ways I can't yet even imagine.

Within an hour I am parking our car three long blocks from the lot full of minivans outside the site of the dance. Nicole, who always whines about the hikes from my remote parking spots, this time makes the trek without a single complaint. Our bodies are both covered with goosebumps—hers from excitement, mine from fear.

"Hey!" a pony-tailed first-grader yells to Nikki as we make our way to the front door. The two of them run to greet one another and nearly plow down some other kid along the way.

"Nicole Lynn, watch where you're—" I stop myself mid-sentence, realizing how futile my protective impulses are going to be for the rest of the night.

Nicole and I make our way inside, but not before she manages to bang into a wicker archway that somehow defies gravity by remaining upright.

I'm not going to survive this.

The next couple of hours play out like one of those old driver's-ed simulator films, with hazards popping up around every corner. At least a dozen times, I catch myself wanting to suggest to Nicole that it's time to go. But over and over again, I manage to choose not to listen to Doubt. *Generosity. Others* side of the pyramid, *Investment* level.

At long last, the Brownie father-daughter dance is drawing to a close. "One more dance," I tell Nicole, who is probably getting tired of my dragging her off to the farthest, least crowded corner of the room every time she suggests we return to the dance floor. The music starts, and to my great relief the song is a slow one. I take Nikki in my arms and hold her tight. We spin in circles, even play with a dip.

Look at us, I want to whisper in her ear as I survey the floor full of little girls and their daddies. Look at us, baby doll; look what we're doing. I settle instead for "I love you, Nicole."

"I love you too, Daddy," she says, snuggling her little head up to that spot where it meets my stomach. "And Daddy . . ." She pauses, looking up at me now.

"Yeah?"

"Thank you."

■

A full week passes, and despite my gloomy predictions, I do *not* spend the time obsessing about the wicker archway, or the slew of kids Nikki bumped into, or anything else related to the dance. Turns out I'm far too preoccupied with another more pressing matter: my impending reunion with Dad. Passover and Easter are now almost here. For better or worse, my father and I are about to sit down together for the first time since my cable episode began more than a month ago. At long last, I will get the very reassurance I've been craving.

So why, I ask myself, am I such a mess just before we head to my grandfather's place for our annual seder?

April 10. I am as anxious today as I've ever been, counting down the minutes until I can "check" with Dad about the cable episode. I hate that I am so compelled to do so, especially when I can see the compulsion for what it is. Yet I am determined to carry it out with as much dignity as I

can muster. Dad will just have to under-
stand. I am doing this so I can move on
with things. I must accept my current
shortcomings and indulge them as neces-
sary. This doesn't feel right, but it's the
best I can do right now.

It's the whole acceptance debate all over again. Maybe I *had* underestimated my ability to look after Nicole in a room full of wild young kids; I did survive the big dance, after all. But this is different. There is simply no way I'm going to get through the rest of my life without checking with Dad on what feels like the most oppressive obsession I've ever had to battle. Why even attempt to delay the inevitable? Get it over with now and move on. Isn't that really what makes the most sense?

Makes sense to me, I answer myself in a voice that sounds suspiciously like Doubt's.

We spend nearly four hours together at the seder, my father and I. Two hundred and forty minutes—any five of which would suffice for my checking needs. But I can't seem to string together even three of those minutes between all the group time, and the seder ceremony, and Dad's many stories about his grand adventures in Africa. Before I know it, it's ten o'clock and Samantha is tugging on my sleeve telling me we need to get the girls home.

This is entirely unfair, in so many ways.

But no matter, I've still got plan B. Two days from now, Dad and I will have a full afternoon together, when we and the rest of our family spend Easter Sunday with Samantha's mother, Joy, at her place in Napa. I've made it this long. What's another forty-eight hours?

■

Halfway through this next two-day delay, I find myself in Joy's backyard, sprawled out and stargazing by her meandering creek. It's a clear and crisp night in the Napa Valley, and a full moon is casting its glow across everything in my sight. There's a certain stillness to the air that we in suburbia seldom get to experience, a distinct absence of car horns and air conditioning units and all the other hums and buzzes of modern living.

I wish Samantha could be out here with me to take all this in. She, however, is tucked away with Joy and the girls, dyeing eggs, baking pies, getting everything ready for tomorrow.

I suppose I too am getting ready, but in my own way. I am steeling myself for the humiliation I know is coming when I launch into my checking drills with my father and hear my own desperate pleas for reassurance. I am paving the way for the inevitable shame I'll fight for weeks after having again succumbed to my monster.

God, I wish I didn't have to go through all this. What I wouldn't give to have the willpower to not even broach the subject with Dad. What an incredible step forward that would be. For a second or two I actually imagine that possibility. And then I hear myself laughing out loud at the prospect. *Yeah, right. Not a chance*—not when the alternative is sixty more years' worth of cueing up the cable-installation tape, much as I again catch myself doing at this very moment.

For the bazillionth time, I hit the Play button. I watch the familiar images of me drilling the hole and running the cable and squeezing caulking out of a tube. I rewind the tape and start to play it again.

And then I realize something: here I am on my back, staring up at the mighty heavens, and I am seeing nothing of them. I am focusing only on the garbage in my head. And come to think of it, this is what I *always* do. For 172 nights I have forced myself to spend a few minutes under the stars. But why? When is the last time I really even tried to lose myself in those stars instead of using my time beneath them to review a few more of my life-sapping tapes?

Pretty hard to see when you refuse to look. Pretty hard to hear when you refuse to listen.

So that's what I decide to do for the next ten minutes. Look and listen. I lock my eyes on the brightest star I can find. I let my ears filter out all but a nearby owl and a chorus of crickets.

Within a few seconds, thoughts of the cable line pop back into my head, but I refuse to give my attention to them. An image of Dad flashes across the virtual screen strung between my ears, but I refuse to assign my focus to it. Doubt whispers something about me wasting my time and repeats the warning over and over, but I let the words fade away like the drawn-out closing refrain of a '70s pop standard.

And so it goes with one thought after another. I watch them float by like so many clouds crossing the sky on a windy afternoon. I catch myself feeling more in charge than I knew I could be. I note that I am exercising my free will in dismissing all the garbage inside my head. I see that I am choosing which thoughts I give my attention.

Good. And you must also choose where you turn for comfort.

Whoa. Where did *that* one come from?

The thought repeats itself, and I wonder for a second whether Doubt again is messing with me. I break my stare and look away from the star.

But this isn't Doubt's whisper, and I know it. In fact, I'm all but certain that I recognize the source of this thought as the very one that had gently suggested I turn on my car radio, and pencil out a pyramid, and give Carole a call when I did. I have no name for it and its powerful nudges, but because of the depth from which it comes, and because of its seeming alignment with something much bigger than myself, I can't help thinking that perhaps "inner believer" is the label that fits. Maybe not. Maybe this is just the "voice of reason" that normal people are always talking about. The only thing I'm really convinced of is that this calming force—whatever its name—is precisely where I'd choose to turn for strength and comfort, if only that were a choice I could make.

But it is.

I am not staring at a star anymore, or picturing a blue dot in some trancelike meditation. I am not counting my breaths or losing myself in the pulsating rhythms of nature. I am just sitting here in Joy's backyard, fully conscious and aware of everything around me. And yet right here with me is this mysterious whisper of inner guidance.

I let myself bathe in the wonder of it for as long as I can, but soon my thoughts return to my father and my challenge at hand. I think about our relationship over the years and how I've increasingly relied on his reassurance for comfort. I think about how my checking compulsions with Dad have come to represent the very worst of my OCD. And again I think about how great it would be to break my addiction.

"I choose where I turn for comfort. *I* choose where I turn for strength. I choose. *I* choose."

I try on the words for size and think again about how much of my life I've let Doubt direct. I see in my mind the horrific "checking" scenes of so many films Doubt has scripted for me. I close my eyes and try to imagine my future in a *non*-Doubt-directed film. I expect dead air, as we call it in broadcasting. But to my great surprise, the scenes take form easily, as if they've always been there, just lying around on the cutting room floor. There's a sequence of me laughing and playing with Nikki and Bri near a sand castle on a beach. And one of me dancing with Samantha on a hot summer night. There are scenes of me sailing my windsurfer, and scenes of me doing fix-it projects around the house. There's a tape of me emceeing a big station event with kids all around me, and another in which I'm speaking at a lectern about my battles with OCD. In all of these scenes, I am happy and strong and whole.

This is me serving my greater good; I am sure of it.

"*This*," I whisper, "is what I choose."

Suddenly I'm feeling more comfort than any checking fix has ever provided.

Suddenly I can't even imagine talking about cables with my dad tomorrow.

Or ever.

twenty-six

PAUSE

Ever see a movie that haunted you—in a constructive way, that is—for years? One that made you think, really think? One that opened your eyes to some deeper truth you'd never seen before? One that, dare I say it, changed your life forevermore? For me there are two movies that fit this bill: one a Hollywood blockbuster (that I'll get back to shortly), and the other my own "virtual production" of the scene I just shared with you.

For the better part of a decade now, I have tried to make sense of what happened that night and why it had such a profound impact on everything that followed. I still can't say for certain, but I'm pretty sure it had to do with the connecting of dots. It's almost as if this giant crayon appeared out of nowhere and started drawing lines and arrows for me: Here's Dad and all that he's come to represent (A). Here's the comforting support of something deep inside you we'll call your "inner believer" (B). Here's the certainty of a greater good (C). And here's the power of your own free will and belief (D). Now then, see how if you use (D) to choose (B) instead of (A) you can get to (C)?

I confess that today this idea often seems like a convoluted football play on a coach's chalkboard to me, but for at least a few seconds on that night by Joy's creek, it all made perfect sense. And if there's one thing I'm convinced of it's that dots once connected are forever joined, even if we lose sight of the lines again and again.

I can't remember just how visible those lines were on April 21, 1998, but I do know from my tapes that I spent much of that particular day trying to connect some other dots on my own. . . .

PLAY Exactly six months down. Exactly six months to go. Halfway there, wherever *there* might be.

It's a Tuesday morning, about nine thirty. The house is empty and quiet as I sit at my den desk poring over the hundreds of index cards spread out in front of me. I am looking for answers, trying to make sense of everything that's happened since my thirty-fourth birthday.

I am getting nowhere.

My index cards read like a mathematical cosine. One day I boast of being on top of the world, the next I use the most dire language possible to describe the depths of my hell. One day I list three items on my episodes cards; the next day twelve. Up and down, and up and down again. Week after week after week. I suppose, to a large degree, this is simply life with OCD. But I know if I dig deep enough, there's got to be more.

And there is.

After an hour or so, I find what I'm looking for: a trend line of sorts—one that's clearly pointing in the right direction. Day 156 has, in fact, proven to be the low point of these past six months. Easter Eve by the creek was, in fact, a quantum leap forward, one that has kept me from even wanting to check with my father on anything OCD-related ever since. I can't explain any of this, but it's all right there on the cards.

Unfortunately, also right there on my cards is evidence of another clear trend—one toward something Jackie has been warning me about. She calls it *scrupulosity*, and in my typical fashion, I've been researching everything I can on the subject, largely in the book *The Doubting Disease*. I've learned that the term itself refers to the notion of imagining sin where it doesn't exist, and that people have been struggling with this sort of thing forever. Way back in the 1600s, in fact, spiritual heavyweight and *Pilgrim's Progress* author John Bunyan wrote an entire book (titled *Grace Abounding*) dealing with his battles with blasphemous thoughts. And a century before him, Martin Luther spoke and wrote of his need to confess several times every day. It seems pastoral counselors have long had to deal with overly scrupulous parishioners, especially within the Catholic church, where structured religious rituals are commonplace and encouraged. I can't help feeling a bit amused reading this, thinking about how often I've secretly wished I were Catholic so I could confess my wrongdoings on a regular basis. *Forgive me, Father, for I have sinned. It's been thirty seconds since my last confession . . .*

Armed with my Jackie warnings, my new research, and personal experience dating all the way back to my potato-bug episode as a kid, I *should* be able to recognize my scrupulosity issues when they come up these days. But like everything else with OCD, it's only in hindsight that I can be that objective. It's only now, as I read through my notes, that I can look back on my moral concerns and see how twisted I can let them become—like just last week when Kitty and I went down to Monterey with our spouses to pick up a big award from the Radio-Television News Directors Association of Northern California. Samantha and I wound up at an Embassy Suites hotel, and for forty-eight hours I fought the urge to pay someone there for the free buffet breakfast a friend and I had helped ourselves to after a meeting at another Embassy Suites nearly *ten* years ago. If Sam had let me, I would have explained all this to the guy at the front desk and laid down a ten-dollar bill. She didn't, though, and for that I'm thankful today. Now I can see the whole thing for what it was: another blatant attempt by Doubt to ruin what was supposed to be an especially rewarding occasion. I can also understand what Jackie's been saying about my morality-based compulsions for years—that what I tell myself is the "right thing to do" is often nothing more than a selfish attempt to rid myself of my doubt and guilt. Should the guy at Embassy Suites really have to figure out what to do with my ten bucks ten years after the fact, just so I can feel better?

Six months become seven all too quickly, as I step up my efforts to make something of my project before time runs out on it.

I continue to battle scrupulosity issues—like needing to drive back to the grocery store after unpacking a stray pack of gum that the checker must have accidentally tossed in my bag, and feeling compelled to remind a waiter that he'd refilled my coffee in case there's an extra charge—but I'm at least learning to hit the Stop button when Doubt gets me reviewing virtual tapes of scruples issues from my past.

I am, in fact, now standing up to Doubt on a fairly regular basis. It's all about choice, I've decided in the wake of my Easter Eve breakthrough. And I *can* choose not to listen to Doubt.

Doubt with a capital *D* does not exist. I understand this. But for whatever combination of reasons, the whole Doubt-as-Director model seems to be working for me. First, it strikes me as right in line with traditional OCD therapy, which encourages OCs to externalize their disorder and learn to talk back to it. And second, it seems so well suited to my own convictions about the power of free will and our need as humans to overcome some illogical innate fear of our own God-given greatness.

So I go with it.

And then, on June 7, 230 days into my project, I get my first glimpse of what Doubt actually *looks* like.

It's a Sunday evening, and I am in a crowded Sacramento theater watching *The Truman Show*,

Peter Weir's brilliant film about a man who plods through life unaware that his hometown is a giant TV studio filled with Hollywood actors, and that his every move is being watched by millions of viewers. As an often jaded member of the media, I've been eager to see this flick, pitched on its surface as a story about societal voyeurism and the extremes to which media moguls will go in search of ratings. But from the opening credits, it's pretty clear to me what this film is really about: one man's quest to know his true identity.

Here's this guy, Truman Burbank, trudging along on the small island of a city he's afraid to leave, until he can no longer fight some inner nudging to seek something bigger. He attempts to venture out, to expand his horizons and discover his true self. But time and again he is thwarted by a series of hazards and obstacles carefully orchestrated by the show's eccentric director, Christof, who simply can't afford to let Truman get to the truth. The show would be over, his director's job gone.

Sitting here taking in Ed Harris's brilliant portrayal of the cunning and conniving Christof, it hits me like a bucket of cold water thrown in my face: I am watching a multimillion-dollar Technicolor Hollywood depiction of precisely how my own nemesis works.

I am getting my first glimpse of Director Doubt.

On the way home, and in bed, and for days to

follow, I imagine Ed Harris's Christof whenever I find myself taking my cues from Doubt. I can almost see him in his high-tech control room, coordinating with special-effects technicians to create elaborate OCD traps, each designed to keep me from getting off my "island" and closer to the reality of who I am.

It's all so much easier to visualize now, like when I'm at my bathroom sink one Sunday morning, scrubbing away and delaying the family from getting to church. I am lost in my compulsion, entirely incapable of stopping—for church or any other reason—until I get this Christof-like image of Doubt in my head. I can almost hear Ed Harris barking orders over a PA to his crew: *"Attention Control Room personnel. Doubt here. Jeff is heading off to church where he'll again be reminded that he's more than his fears and his doubts. We can't let that happen. We need to drill into him that his hands aren't clean. We need to keep him from ever leaving this house."*

In one of *The Truman Show*'s most powerful scenes, Christof explains to a reporter that he's in charge of Truman's life only because Truman, not knowing better, lets him "direct" it. As Christof proclaims with great arrogance in response to one of the reporter's questions, "We accept the reality of the world with which we're presented."

Slowly but surely, I am coming to understand

that that very statement is at the crux of every one of my OCD problems.

I am also beginning to realize one other thing: I, like Truman, have been living on an island—a moving one with Samantha at its center. Sam is my OCD safety net, and I am so dependent on her that I can't even risk being out of her range. What would happen if she weren't around to drive me when I'm incapable of getting behind the wheel, or scoop me off of the bathroom floor when I'm emotionally unable to get up by myself? How would I ever get by without Sam to cover for me when I'm about to get caught in an OCD ritual, or to talk me out of pursuing some god-awful compulsion I'll later regret? I can't even imagine the answers. So I refuse to let myself even think about being very far from my wife at any given time.

Samantha says I'm underestimating myself.

"I think you should go on the AOU retreat," she tells me one Sunday on the way home from church. She's talking about the annual "Adults of Unity" retreat back in Kansas City, Missouri. A dozen or so people from our local church are going this year.

"Yeah, sure," I say, dismissing the idea outright.

"Think about it. What could be a safer environment than a church retreat? It would be so good for you."

Samantha's right on both counts, and I know it. At her insistence, I agree to talk to Wayne Manning, who used to work at the Unity Village retreat grounds and still makes regular visits out there. Wayne, knowing my fear of inflicting damage, promises to pass along a list of every hazard I've left behind in Missouri as soon as I get home. I send in my registration the following day.

So now I am plotting an escape from my island, and Doubt is pissed off and determined to make sure I stay put. Like Christof scrambling to keep Truman from getting away, my cerebral enemy begins setting one trap after another to scare me into changing my plans. Scruples issues. Germ issues. Driving issues. Hazard issues. My OCD attacks double by the day.

But it's too late. My airfare is paid for, my retreat deposit nonrefundable.

I can't even imagine how this movie will end.

twenty-seven

fast-forward 2 weeks

Nine hours, two flights, one shuttle ride, and a half-dozen OCD episodes after leaving Sacramento, I arrive at Unity Village. I am exhausted and need a nap in the worst kind of way.

I check in, and the lady at the registration desk directs me to a long motel-like building at the edge of the retreat grounds. Quaint and rustic, I'm guessing, is how most guests would describe this dilapidated wooden building built back in the 1950s. But "old" and "vulnerable" are the first two adjectives I come up with as I haul my bags into my room.

I have my own small bathroom—a big, big

plus—and the first thing I do is check the flow of the toilet. It's the first thing I always check. Better to know at the onset what kind of problems I'm likely to have with clogs and overflows and various flushing issues. My test toilet paper scrap seems to go down just fine. But I can hear a steady drip coming from the nearby shower. Turns out it's the hot water valve; it won't shut off completely. I should report this right away. But I challenge myself to wait until tomorrow or maybe the day after that.

The rest of the room is pretty much what I'd expected: a couple of twin beds, a small desk, two nightstands, and a back door leading to the retreat grounds' main pathways. Everything seems to be in working order. No loose electrical sockets or sagging towel racks or other hazards I'll need to fix or report.

According to my activity schedule, lunch is still being served in the cafeteria for another ten minutes, so I decide to make my way over there for a bite. But I can't seem to get the back door open. At first I think I must be missing some kind of a latch or deadbolt. Then I realize the whole door is swollen— or perhaps, painted—shut. *Maybe we're not supposed to use these rear doors.* I look out the window and see one back door after another open and close. I give mine one more tug. Nothing. No way am I going to try pulling any harder than that. I have visions of collapsing the entire old building.

I'll just go around the long way all week, I decide.

I get my first glimpse of the sprawling retreat grounds on my way to the cafeteria. Lush green lawns as far as I can see in every direction—1,400 acres worth, I think I read. There are two lakes, an oversized pool, tennis courts, a golf course, and a world-famous rose garden. The place has a college-campus feel, with crisscrossing pathways connecting a dozen or so Mediterranean-style buildings. Very serene. Very tranquil.

As for our itinerary, it's supposed to be entirely open-ended. The retreat brochure promised a mix of planned activities and free time, with participants free to choose whatever balance of the two that they'd like. I'm thinking I'd be perfectly happy hanging out in my safe room the entire time.

But I don't. I force myself to go to the general assembly after lunch and scout things out. There are people of all ages filling the room. Lots of couples and large groups of friends. More women than men by a factor of at least two to one. I feel like the odd guy out. And that's even before I start with any of my OCD oddities.

It's well after eleven by the time we wrap up all the afternoon orientations and dinner and an evening concert. I can't wait to get my head on my pillow, and the two come together like opposite poles of a magnet. I am exhausted. Too exhausted to even give more than a passing thought to the sticking back door, and the dripping shower faucet, and the small tear I noticed on the seat of the airplane, and the lamp that I bumped into on my way into bed.

Jackie would call this OCD flooding.

Our first full day at the Village is a Sunday. We're encouraged to spend at least half of it wandering the grounds and learning our way around. I am again tempted to stay in my room, but I've spent far too much money on this trip to let that happen. I know I need to do what I came here for. I have got to find ways to push myself, and the obvious one is just down the road. I put on my swim trunks and sandals and head to the nearby swimming pool I've been hearing about.

The air here in Missouri is sticky with a wet summer heat that we in the West know nothing about, and the idea of diving into a pond of cool, crystal clear water is highly inviting, to say the least. But I have a problem. For at least three years now, I have found it next to impossible to get myself into a public pool. For that I can thank Doubt, always ready with one deadly contamination scenario or another to scare me away. My sweat, a splash of urine on my leg, the bacteria from my athlete's foot or jock itch infections: there are so many hypothetical sources of trouble.

Today it's a new one. Today it's the brightly colored braid of embroidery thread around my wrist. The girls made it for me as a "friendship bracelet" to keep us together in our time apart. They are wearing similar ones this week, and there's no way I can take mine off.

But what if the ink from the thread bleeds into the pool?

"Yeah, what if!" I want to shout back at Doubt at the top of my lungs. Instead I just stand frozen at the edge of the pool, trying to look casual but shaking inside like one of those paint-mixing machines. I've got to believe that anyone watching me must think I'm terrified of drowning. How could they know that my fear is not what the water could do to me, but rather what I could do to the water?

Minutes, hours, and days seem to pass as I stand by the pool. People come and go. One lifeguard leaves and another takes over. And still I just stand there. Doubt won't let me jump in. Something deep inside won't let me walk away. I am frozen in place, incapable of budging an inch. Not even the blazing Midwest sun can break my freeze.

But then in an instant and without any warning, something does melt through the fear that has me paralyzed. It's a soft and gentle nudge, the source of which I cannot see, and it's followed by the sweetest sounding splash I have ever heard.

■

Fourteen hours later, it's the sound of a crash, not a splash, that grabs my attention. It's the middle of the night, but the sky outside my window is brighter than any glaring Sacramento afternoon in the hottest stretch of the summer.

And then, in a heartbeat, it is pitch dark again.

I am still only half awake when the next booming crash rattles the glass just inches from me. Again the sky comes alive with intense zigzags of light stretching from east to west, and west to east, and every other combination of compass points possible.

This is, I gather, an authentic Midwest thunderstorm. It is the most spectacular sight I have ever seen. Lightning in urban Northern California comes in single vertical distant discharges. Nothing at all like this. I am mesmerized. Like a kid watching his first snowfall, I sit with my nose glued to the window. For at least an hour I soak it all in. I marvel at the wonders of nature, and I marvel at the past forty-eight hours. I watch the darkness turn to light and I think about my swim in the pool. I watch the sleeping heavens come alive, and I think about my escape from the island.

I can't remember the last time I felt so awake. So invigorated. So filled with possibility. I want to go outside and lie down in the grass (until I realize how asinine that would be during a thunderstorm). I want to call Sam and the girls and tell them I love them. I want to put on loud music and sing along and dance until I'm dizzy. I want to pound my chest and let loose a primeval yell. I want to live.

I want to live.

That's it right there, I suppose. For the first time in years, I *want* to be alive.

■

I am a different person the next two days, someone other than the guy who checked himself into my room. This someone is making himself a part of the AOU retreat—meeting people, taking hikes in the woods, even signing up to read a couple of old poems in the annual talent show, despite Doubt's insistence that I consider whether my original prose might in fact be something less than original. *Can you really be sure you didn't somehow plagiarize the material? What if you lifted a line or two from some other poem you'd read and didn't even know it?*

The week is half over before I know it, and I have yet to report a single hazard, yet to ask for reassurance from a single soul. Samantha and I talk on the phone every night, and I always hang up with teeth marks in my tongue from having fought so hard to avoid bringing up one concern or another.

At least once a day I find myself thinking about *The Truman Show* and one scene in particular when Truman is about to bust out forever from the studio bubble that has been his home. And then one afternoon it dawns on me that I myself have one final exit I have yet to break through, one I'm standing no more than five feet from at the moment.

I make my way over to the back door of my room. I put my hand on the doorknob and close my eyes.

You won't do it. You don't have the guts. It's Christof taunting Truman. Doubt taunting me.

I tighten my grip on the knob. I grit my teeth.

I'll make you pay the price for this forever. You'll be playing back tapes of this moment for as long as you live.

Arggggggghhhhhh. I pull at the door with every ounce of my strength. The walls groan like a wrestler about to be pinned. The windows rattle. The ceiling shakes as if hit by an earthquake.

And then the door is open.

And then I am standing on the other side.

And then Doubt is nowhere to be heard.

■

Among Unity Village's more popular attractions is a colossal labyrinth patterned after a famous medieval one in France's Chartres Cathedral. It looks to me like a giant version of one of those circular mazes you draw as a kid. But the retreat directors insist it's a powerful tool for walking meditations, and at lunch one afternoon, the AOUers I'm sitting with are going on about how wonderful it is. "I'll have to try it out," I say, just attempting to be polite. But then a woman named Cathleen turns to me and suggests we get together after the evening program to give it a go. I can't think of any inherent OCD hazards, nor can I come up with any excuses off the top of my head, so I say "sure" and arrange to touch base later.

We meet up that night just as the Kansas City sun is slipping away for the day. I know nothing about Cathleen except that we both hail from Sacramento. She's in her forties, I'm guessing, and is traveling with a woman who also shares our home city.

The two of us start tackling the mammoth concentric circles, weaving our way back and forth, moving ever toward the decorative center. A handful of other retreat-goers are also walking the labyrinth, and instead of focusing on my footsteps or my breath or anything else even remotely rhythmic, I am keeping a close mental inventory of just where everyone is; I can't afford to go plowing into any of my fellow spiritual seekers. I am getting nothing meaningful out of this whatsoever, but the way I figure it, I *am* at least getting some exercise.

We finish up and Cathleen asks, "So what do you think?"

"Interesting," I say, not wanting to burst her bubble.

"Somebody told me the best way to experience these things is with your eyes closed," she says.

"Huh?"

"Well, of course, you have to have someone with you, guiding you along."

"Oh, I see," I say. I do. But I don't like where this conversation is going.

"Whadda ya say? You up for it?" What *can* I say? The next thing I know I'm walking in circles with my eyes closed, Cathleen's right hand on my left shoulder. I am scared to death. *What if Cathleen runs me right into some other labyrinth walker out here. Wouldn't it still be my fault?* I want to cheat but I'm afraid of getting caught. I want this to be over. I simply can't trust her.

"Isn't this a great exercise in trust?" I hear Cathleen whisper at that moment. I wonder if she's somehow picking up on how nervous I am.

She's on to my dirty secret, I decide by the time we wrap up this tortuous drill and make our way to a nearby bench. I need to be careful here. She's from

Sacramento, after all, and who's to say she won't go spreading my dirt all over town.

We start talking about the retreat and Wayne and Carole and our other mutual connections back home. We discover our two rooms at the motel share a common wall, and wonder out loud what the chances of that were.

"So how'd you wind up getting involved with our church, anyway?" Cathleen wants to know.

"Oh, it's a long story," I say, almost dismissively.

"Yeah? I'd love to hear it."

Now what to do? There are so many contrived stories I've resorted to in the past. But I can't seem to bring myself to lie to this woman. Maybe it's this exercise in trust we've just finished. Maybe it's having spent the past several days attempting to live with at least some authenticity for once.

Maybe it's just that knowing look on her face.

"I was going through some pretty tough years when I found our church," I say.

Cathleen nods her head, makes it clear I need say nothing at all more than that.

But this is a test, or at least an opportunity, my intuition is telling me. I'm supposed to try talking about my OCD here. Supposed to see how it feels and whether I can do it. So I do. For the first time in my life, I share my secret with someone with no ties, professional or otherwise, to the OCD or recovery worlds. Even my closest friends and relatives know nothing of what I hear myself telling this woman I've known for less than a day. By the time I am done, I have shared with Cathleen every iota of my story.

There's a long pause when I run out of words. I am standing naked now in a busy street with people in windows high above looking down and gawking at me.

I close my eyes. Because I can't bear to look at Cathleen. Because it's the only way I know to make the world disappear.

"Thank you," Cathleen whispers. "Thank you for trusting me with all that."

I can't speak at this moment. But if I could, I'd tell her that it's I who should be saying thanks. Because, while I'm not sure I understand the significance, I know I have just taken the first, and perhaps most difficult, step in going public with my story. And for this, I know that I'll forever be indebted to Cathleen. I also know that she, like Carole Johnson, didn't fall into my project by chance.

■

My emotions are raw and at the surface the entire next day. Whatever thick skin I had left on my body is now just tissue paper that continues to tear. Fortunately for my self-esteem, I'm not the only one fighting to keep things together. It seems half the people around me are bawling their eyes out time and again. Lots of folks dealing with lots of issues in this safe environment. I suppose that's why most of us are here.

By nightfall we are all in desperate need of a break, and our retreat directors must know this. They arrange for a Sufi dance instructor to teach us some moves. Most of us look downright goofy going through the motions, but no one cares. We are all just unwinding, trying to have some fun before our scheduled twelve-hour exercise in silence, which we kick off at nine with a group labyrinth walk. In a giant Congo line, we snake our way back and forth through the giant maze. When it's over we head back to our rooms in a collective hush. The only sounds anywhere are coming from the Village's natural habitat.

That is, until I get about halfway home and look down at my pants.

My fly is wide open. I mean *wiiiiide* open.

For a second or two I am paralyzed with fear. But then the irony hits me: Could there have been a worse time to get caught with my zipper down? There I was dancing with at least a hundred people in a giant circle, switching partners every few minutes. And just in case anyone happened to miss the white of my underpants peeking clear as day through my khaki shorts, what do I do? I parade past each and every one of them, again and again, as we make our way back and forth, and back and forth, and back and forth, through the labyrinth.

I am a kid in church now who sees something hanging out of the pastor's nose, but knows the commotion he'll cause if he lets himself laugh as he's dying to. The entire Village is silent. Even the crickets are mute tonight. But I am snickering under my breath and there's so much more I need to let out.

I do just that—let it all out—when I get back to my room. I start laughing so hard that my gut starts to ache. So hard that my eyes are pouring over with tears. So hard that I can only imagine what Cathleen and her roommate and the people on the other side of my room must be thinking.

So hard that I start thinking about how many years it's been since I've let out a laugh of any size at all.

■

The retreat continues for another full day, but before I know it, we're all packing our bags and saying goodbye. Cathleen and I swap phone numbers and promise to get together back in Sacramento. We discuss the irony of traveling to a retreat more than a thousand miles from home with a hundred-plus people from dozens of states, and each finding that the one person we most want to stay in touch with is someone from our home city that we didn't even know. What are the chances?

I leave Unity Village without reporting my door or my shower or the spider I killed.

I leave thinking this was the best investment—financial and otherwise—that I have ever made.

I leave knowing that I have found everything I was looking for here.

◼

Three hours later I discover I was wrong. It seems there is at least one other thing I was supposed to find.

I am standing in a waiting area in the Kansas City Airport when I put all this together. I am killing time before my flight back to California, staring at a pamphlet on the floor and shaking my head. Thirty seconds ago this pamphlet had been ten feet away from me. Out of habit, really, I started wondering whether someone might slip on it and fall. I knew I couldn't pick it up, not after all the progress I'd made this past week. But then I noticed the three words printed on its two-by-five-inch cover: *The Golden Key*. Intriguing, I had to admit after a week like this past one. I walked over for a closer look and discovered that this brochure was, of all things, a Unity reprint of an old Emmet Fox article. Fox has been my favorite "New Thought" writer for years. I have a boxed anthology of his work in my den, and I was rereading one of his books the very day I left Sacramento. So this is all a little too coincidental again.

Now, I want to pick up the brochure and read through its contents, but Doubt reminds me that it will then be my responsibility forever and ever. I certainly can't put it back on the floor, and *what if it belongs to someone who will be missing it soon?*

Curiosity wins. I retrieve the pamphlet and flip through its pages, knowing in an instant that it was destined for me all along. How could it not have been? Here in my hands, in the most clear and concise language I have yet to run across, is what Emmet Fox calls a "scientific prayer" technique aimed at keeping users from dwelling on their worries.

The key, he advises, is to drive distressing thoughts out of one's consciousness by *replacing* them, if only for a few moments, with thoughts of God (truth, wisdom, and love, for example). Big troubles, little troubles: it's entirely possible, he says, to "golden key" them all with this thought-substitution process.

Damn. Isn't this a spiritual application of the very same refocusing technique that Dr. Jeffrey Schwartz and other OCD specialists advocate? Is this not a practical means by which an OC like myself can manually do what my faulty caudate nucleus is supposed to, but cannot, do for me automatically—namely switch gears, move on, change the subject? And isn't Fox's essay, written way back in 1931, presenting all this as a simple, willful choice between thoughts of doubt and thoughts of what I've come to think of as the higher power behind a greater good?

For years now, I've been trying to reconcile my traditional OCD therapy with my slowly growing understanding of spiritual principles. I have struggled to explain to Jackie and other mental health professionals just how helpful "practical spirituality" has been for me in dealing with my obsessions and compulsions. Likewise, I have had only limited success making sense of traditional behavior therapy for Wayne and others in the clergy. Somehow it's always struck me that the two professions are speaking different languages—describing similar principles, but in very different tongues.

As far as I'm concerned, this is the link that puts it all together. Perhaps I shouldn't need this validation of my personal approach to my OCD recovery, but I do.

And *now,* it seems, I have found everything I went looking for in Kansas City.

twenty-eight

fast-forward 5 hours

Samantha and the girls pick me up at Sacramento International. Anyone watching the reception they give me might think I've just returned from a tour of duty in some foreign battle zone. In a lot of ways, I suppose I have.

It's great to be back home, but as I begin unpacking my stuff and settling in, I can't help noticing this weird time-warp phenomenon. A mere week has gone by for my family, but a seeming eternity has passed for me. My world has been turned upside down and back again, and it doesn't seem possible that this has all happened in just seven days. I am not the same person my wife and daughters said goodbye to last Friday, nor will I ever be again. Yet nothing, *nothing,* has changed here at home. Sam and the girls look just the same, the weather is just as I remember it, the newspaper is following the same stories that I myself had covered before leaving, and the mail on my desk is right where I left it.

And then there's the whole issue of attempting to convey my experience in Missouri. Do I even try? How does one go about telling someone—even his own wife—about a life-changing thunderstorm? Or about a pamphlet he found with *The Golden Key?* The short answer seems to be, you don't. I reason there will be plenty of time later. It's all right there on my index cards, if and when I ever have the nerve.

■

Cathleen calls a couple days later to see how I'm doing "back in the real world."

I'm not sure. It's been a tough adjustment, tougher than I'd anticipated, returning to all the chaos that is my daily life in Sacramento. My spirits are up. My attitude is in the right place. But any delusions I might have had about leaving my OCD back in Missouri are now ancient history. I've already battled my way though several episodes since returning and have caught myself reviewing a handful of tapes. Still, for what it's worth, I'm finding that my checking drills now *feel* "wrong." Any quick relief they bring me is more than countered by a sense of having sold myself short. I guess it's the *integrity* part of my believing pyramid.

Carole and I kick all this around a few days later. She wants to hear every last detail about Unity Village. Carole may be the one person in my world who fully understands what my trip was all about. She herself has not traveled outside of Sacramento more than a half-dozen times over the past ten years. Too many OCD challenges, even with her husband, Bud, right by her side. If only vicariously, Carole wants to take in this magical place in Missouri she's heard so much about.

She wants to make sure I'm getting it all down in print.

There's nothing like counting days to make you appreciate the fleeting nature of time. Of the 365 I've committed to my project, exactly 265 of them have now passed and are recorded for posterity on the cards stacked in front of me. Some quick math tonight tells me a mere hundred days remain. This is sobering. It wasn't all that long ago that a year seemed like an eternity, more than enough time to get a handle on my OCD and turn my life around.

But now October 21 is staring me right in the face. The pressure is on, and I'm feeling it.

It's time to get serious.

It's time to put into practice everything I've been working on with my believing model—not just some of the time, but all of the time.

It's time to start holding the line on my compulsions—the checking, the tape reviewing, the confessing, the hand-washing, the reassurance seeking—not only when I'm feeling strong, but even when I'm not.

It's time to push myself harder with each passing day.

Notching up the discomfort—that's what Jackie always used to call it. She's thrilled to hear *me* using the term now in a phone session as I describe my plans for the coming three months. She's also duly impressed when I recite my laundry list of accomplishments from the Kansas City trip.

"Good, Jeff!" she says, again and again.

In our three years together, I can't think of a time I've felt better at the end of our fifty minutes.

■

I start counting down the days on my calendar. Ninety-nine, ninety-eight, ninety-seven, ninety-six . . . I force myself to go through an entire afternoon without playing back an aircheck in search of missed spots. I drag myself to the self-serve soda fountain and get my own drink. I leave the corner of a curled-up floor mat just as I found it.

Ninety-five, ninety-four, ninety-three, ninety-two . . .

I pass on my nightly "checking time" with Sam. I take a trip to San Francisco with Cathleen and several friends and survive five trips to public bathrooms. I invite a co-worker out to lunch and offer to drive.

▪

One hundred days become thirty before I know it. Now there is only one month to go. It's time again to notch up the discomfort. I am still "cheating" too much, finding far too many clever and subtle ways to get my checking fixes, especially from Sam. So I pull her aside on September 21 and tell her I won't be asking her opinion about anything for the next thirty days.

"Okay," she says, more than a little amused.

"It's the only way," I explain.

"I won't be insulted."

I can tell she's not taking me seriously.

"Just look away if I ask you about anything," I tell her. "If I ask you whether you think I'm ready to tackle this or that, or if I ask you whether you agree I've handled something or another correctly. Even if

I ask you whether my blue tie works with my pin-striped Oxford."

"You got it," my wife says, and I can only wonder what's going through her head.

Later in my den, I make another commitment as well. I promise myself I will go out of my way to tackle at least ten OCD challenges every day. I will note them on the back of my index cards with little triangles, just as Nicole and her Girl Scout friends collect triangular "Try-It" badges on their scouting vests.

It's another little game, but it quickly proves effective. Day after day, I fill up the backs of my cards with tiny triangles. I put one down for the piece of plywood I drive over without doubling back to check on. I put one down for the paperback I return to a shelf at Barnes & Noble after perusing with my germ-infested hands. I put one down for the small puddle of Pepsi that I don't report to the guy behind the hot dog counter.

It's not long before I'm running out of three-by-five space for all my index card Try-It notes.

■

On the first Saturday in October, the station throws a company picnic by the river, and the girls and I make what I figure to be a quick appearance. We eat hot dogs and chat with a few friends, then I'm ready to go. But Janice from accounting is walking around signing up people for the three-legged race. Sam, almost sarcastically, dares me to give it a try with her. She thinks I'm kidding when I take off after Janice to grab one of the ties. But five minutes later, there we are banging into everyone with our legs bound together. The wheelbarrow race is next and my kid-at-heart wife decides to push her luck. "How could it be any worse?" she argues. So I agree to give it a go.

We come in second. Smash into another tandem along the way. Laugh at the absurdity of it all.

Tangled up with me at the finish line, Sam whispers, "If I didn't know better, I'd think you were having fun."

She's right. And I can't even think of the last time anyone might have caught me "having fun." There just hasn't been a lot of room for such a luxury amidst all of Doubt's demands.

But maybe this is a turning point. Maybe I am back in the game in more ways than one.

twenty-nine

fast-forward 18 days

10:45 p.m., Day 365.

I am sitting at my den desk, agonizing over the precise words that should occupy the last fifteen square inches of lined white space in front of me. The right words to button up this big experiment of mine.

Nothing comes to me.

I take a minute to look around my den at my many treasured mementos of the past twelve months. On my wall: a framed color photo of Unity Village that Cathleen had enlarged for me. On my shelves: at least two dozen thoroughly highlighted new books covering everything from traditional psychology to practical spirituality, along with my dog-eared Emmet Fox treasure from the floor of the Kansas City airport. And on my desk: a well-weathered cardboard pyramid and thousands of neatly stacked and categorized index cards just waiting for *one* more to forever join their ranks.

I begin pulling out, looking over, and trying to make sense of my three-by-five cards. There are so many of them now, each like a thumbnail snapshot at a multimedia Web site—"Click here to watch a streaming video of this image." I do this because that's how my head works, and because that's the only way I know how to process the events of my life. But my playbacks tonight are my own. It is I, and not Doubt, in charge of what images I see and how many times I choose to review them. Easily and without even a hint of anxiety, I shuffle from one scene to another—from my dip in the pool in Missouri to Nicole's father-daughter dance, from the moonlit creek in Joy's backyard to the recent company picnic. Sequence after sequence, I play back my tapes from the past 365 days, and then from the five years before them. The Boat. The bouncing body. The call to the coroner. Dr. X. Dr. Y. Dr. Z. Dr. Smith. Dr. Schwartz. Jackie. The pills. The exposures. My virtual asylum. My bargain with the stars . . .

My Bargain with the Stars—not much chance of glossing over that one on this night.

Oct. 20, 1998. And so ends one journey as another begins.

Now I have eight words on my index card, and it strikes me right away that they are not at all the ones I would have expected to wind up there. Day 365 was supposed to be about closure, not transitions; about walking out of a building into a field, not stepping through a narrow doorway separating one room from another. I know there's another big project awaiting my attention, and I know it involves the very same cards now spread across my desk. I understand that what lies ahead is nothing short of a journey in and of itself, and I can now admit that I'm excited about that. But I guess it's the "baggage" I'm taking with me that has me questioning everything. Wasn't I supposed to be leaving all my obsessions and compulsions at the door marked Exit?

Wasn't I supposed to be done forever with my OCD?

Sitting here tonight, I know this will not be the case, and for proof I need only look over the handful of items on my most recent episodes cards. I also know better than to be surprised. I understand, if only intellectually, that I can no more be cured of my brain disorder than a former drunk can be cured of his alcoholism. Much as he'll always be one drink away from a night in the gutter, I suppose *I* will forever be one OCD episode away from my own personal hell. That illusory asylum of mine will always be waiting for me at the end of my virtual tapes.

I am, and forever will be, an obsessive-compulsive.

Ahh, so you finally admit it!

I've been waiting for Doubt to check in one last time during my project—waiting and challenging myself to hold my own on this all-important night. I know what's coming.

Toss the cards.

I close my eyes.

Toss the cards and admit it's all over. You failed.

No.

Admit it, you FAILED!

No.

This whole "project" of yours, wasn't it all about getting over OCD?

Maybe not.

Yeah, right! Then what was it about?

I have the answer and I silently shout it: Maybe it was about learning to live with the "discomfort of uncertainty"—as Jackie had put it this morning at the end of what we triumphantly agreed would be our final phone session.

Maybe it was about coming to trust that there's a "greater good" certainty and unlimited resources to help us find it.

Maybe it was about claiming my natural birthright of free will and using it to decide for myself who and what will direct my life.

Maybe it was about accepting that, while I cannot chase you away, Doubt, I *can* choose not to take my directions from you.

Silence.

Nothing now from Doubt, and this feels like such a sweet victory.

I grab my pen . . .

What was it I wrote one year ago tonight?
Something like "my outcome is certain
or my premise eternally flawed." With
the same certainty I claimed back then, I
can now report that my premise—that we
have within us the "tools" to transform our
lives—is far from flawed. It is the greatest
truth I will ever know.

PAUSE So here's where I'm going to need to mess with time, to somehow morph the guy in my final 1998 project tapes with the guy writing these words in 2006. I have to do this because after hours of trying to separate what I knew then from what I know now, I've decided I can't. Not even with the help of virtual tapes and index cards. Still, I want to share with you this "greatest truth I will ever know." The painfully obvious one about the "tools" we have to transform our lives. The one I came to understand that night. The one I have lived by ever since.

So simple, really: those tools, they are nothing more than our choices—the ones we make a thousand times a day, and the ones that, strung together, define our lives.

I know this because of all that happened during the 365 days of my *crash course in believing*. Nothing magic, in retrospect. Nothing even very profound. Just an application, really, of so many seemingly divergent approaches to dealing with uncertainty through the power of our choices. Jackie's coaching. Cognitive behavioral therapy. Jerry Jampolsky's dueling directors. Dr. Schwartz's impartial spectators and refocusing techniques. My little cardboard pyramid. So many ways of applying the same fundamental principles of free will and belief. So many life lessons learned along the way.

The triumphs, the setbacks, the breakthroughs, the steps forward and backward on my road to recovery: all of them, I know now, were the results of my own willful application—or lack thereof—of the myriad teachings and resources made available to me. I also know now that out of the alchemy of my one-year project came a set of very specific tools I could use to cope with the day-to-day challenges of life with OCD, tools that have served me incredibly well for nearly a decade now.

The catch with OCD coping skills is that they're entirely individual. Because of the wide spectrum of OCD challenges, and the unique life circumstances that each and every obsessive-compulsive brings to recovery, I'm not sure there can ever be a one-size-fits-all approach to battling this disorder. With that said, though, I do want to share with you here my *own* personal approach to living with OCD—first, because it's such an integral part of my story, and second, because I'm convinced the core strategies and principles I've drawn on are fundamental to any OC's recovery efforts.

So here goes:

Keep Perspective.
Take Initiative.
Release and Have Faith.

Keep Perspective.
OCD obsessions are irrational, and they're the result of false messages sent by malfunctioning brains. This is fact. But try convincing an obsessive-

compulsive in the throes of some horrific episode! In those critical moments, our fears—whether killing off swimmers in a pool with dye leaked from a thread, or causing a pedestrian landmine with a piece of a Reese's Peanut Butter Cup—are very, very real to us. It's only by cultivating perspective that we're able to step back and see how illogical our concerns are. As any OC will tell you, this is no easy task.

Fortunately, there are some powerful, proven techniques for gaining this perspective. Dr. Jeffrey Schwartz, for example, advises OCs to recognize and "relabel" obsessions and compulsions. So when I run over a pothole and begin imagining that I might have unknowingly plowed someone down, I should force myself to say (out loud or in my head): "I am obsessing that I've run over some poor soul in the street" *and* "I'm fighting a compulsion to loop my car around to look for signs of an accident."

Next, Schwartz suggests OCs "reattribute" these challenges, to acknowledge that they're the medical result of biochemical issues with the brain, and *not* a rational concern needing our attention. While this technique is far more easily said than accomplished, it is, with time and practice, an amazingly effective tool, and it has worked wonders in my own recovery.

Perspective, too, is an OC's means to another

important end: understanding the *real* motives behind our compulsions. As Jackie was so skilled at pointing out to me, Captain Hazard's seemingly magnanimous gestures to save the world were, far more often than not, nothing more than feeble attempts to save *himself* from future agony. Take the time I reported a few drips of water from my umbrella to the gal behind the Safeway checkout stand, prompting a code-seven alert for aisle three. After attempting to convince Jackie that it wasn't *that* strange that the kid with the mop couldn't *find* the "puddle," I had to concede that, yeah, I guess I inconvenienced the store crew; and, yeah, I guess I did it so I wouldn't have to replay tapes of the whole thing later on.

For me, finding perspective with OCD also involves a much bigger picture. It's about coming to understand that there's a "greater good" in every situation, and that in pursuit of these bigger-picture ideals, sacrifices (most notably, in comfort) often need to be made. When I "broke through" the stuck door at Unity Village, for example, I knew I'd obsess about potential damage later. But I also knew that a triumph this big would go a long way in helping me get my life back on track, and therefore would help me become a better husband, father, friend. Time and again, keeping sight of a greater good has allowed me to find inner strength I didn't know I had.

Take Initiative.

Here's an unfortunate but important reality about battling OCD: It's hard work. Really, really, really hard work. And there are no shortcuts. Period.

This is a lesson I've had to learn for myself, and I suspect that's the case with many, if not most, OCs. I spent at least a year sitting in Jackie's office week after week, taking in her advice and nodding my head, then all but ignoring that advice between our appointments. Cognitive behavioral therapy works. I know this for a fact today. But no amount of therapy, no matter how proven, can really do an OC any good, *until* he or she is ready to take the initiative to implement its techniques.

What's so significant about my Unity Village trip, I'm now convinced, is that it marked the beginning of my serious commitment to "do the hard work." I may be the only person ever to have gone on a spiritual retreat with dozens of peace-seekers, only to stress myself out intentionally. But then again, I now know that I too was working on my own peace, albeit one near-panic-attack at a time.

At the core of OCD behavior therapy is the practice of exposure/response prevention (ERP) which, as I described earlier, centers on the notion of working to prevent compulsive responses to obsessive thoughts by delaying them in increasing durations. Without calling it out as such, I spent my week in Missouri doing just this. By exposing myself to one OCD challenge after another, and refusing to give into my compulsive urges to get Sam's phone reassurance and report my concerns to the retreat staff, I sat with the discomfort long enough to get past the worst of it. Again, as the experts point out, it's a desensitization process. Start by getting through one day without reporting the dripping faucet, then challenge myself to get through the week. In the end, I never did feel the need to give Wayne Manning my list of all the items I'd "broken" at the Village.

Delaying and limiting compulsions is tricky business and takes an unbelievable amount of conscious initiative, especially with a compulsion as easy to slip into as mental checking. As I've learned from Dr. Schwartz, active refocusing is definitely the key (the "golden key," as Emmet Fox puts it). When I'm compelled to sit in a room and replay tapes of a lane-change, for example, I force myself to engage my mind in some other activity—usually tackling some writing project. (For years, it's been working on this very book that has saved me time and again!) There is no OCD coping practice that I work with more in my day-to-day life than this one.

Another harsh reality of OCD treatment is that it's not enough to simply *react* to challenges as they come. ERP is most effective when it's done proactively. Trust me, the last thing an OC wants to do is spend time between episodes creating new ones; but that, I've learned from Jackie, is the only way serious progress is made. Over the years, Jackie sent me home with numerous homework assignments, from driving down narrow streets to putting myself in situations in which I couldn't wash. Only when I finally started doing my homework did I begin to learn my own capabilities. Challenging myself is an ongoing process I know I'll never be able to stop without risking relapse.

Like finding perspective, taking initiative in battling OCD is, in my mind, a very life-affirming process. It's claiming and exercising one's innate freedom of choice, and I've learned a great deal about the practice from so many authors who write not about mental health, but about spiritual growth. In his book *Your Sacred Self*, Dr. Wayne Dyer talks extensively about taking initiative through our "willingness" to pursue our goals. Following his lead years ago, I wrote down for myself a series of "willingness commitments" based on my belief model, and I've tried to take the initiative to recite them every day ever since. When I think about *Strength*, for example, I remind myself that I must be willing to "resist reassurance and sacrifice comfort" and "find the courage to meet every challenge."

Willingness and initiative, I've come to understand, go hand in hand.

Release and Have Faith.

One of the great ironies about learning to manage OCD is that to battle your obsessions, you've got to accept them. Anyone who's ever taken the challenge to avoid thinking about, say, purple elephants knows that it's impossible, and that purple elephants will, in fact, consume your mind as you try in vain to do this. Such is the case with obsessions. The more we OCs attempt to fight them off, the more they're certain to lodge themselves front and center in our heads. The answer, I have learned, is to acknowledge, label, and accept obsessions, and in so doing, allow ourselves to release our attachments to them. Seemingly paradoxical, it's another powerful exercise, but it also takes a great deal of faith.

As I explained earlier, obsessions *feel* very real to OCs. To release them requires that we move past chemically based emotion to some deeper level of knowing. For me, this has meant coming to understand that there's a greater good in every moment, and that by tapping into some inner source of strength and comfort (my inner-believer), I can find the faith to move beyond faulty physiology.

Release, for me, is also very much about letting go of the past and the future, maybe the toughest challenge for OCs or anyone struggling with uncertainty. Director Doubt wants me to obsess over past mistakes and what horrific things they'll mean for the future. Only through release can I attempt to find peace in the present. Sometimes it takes a bolt of lightning (literally, as I found in Missouri) to snap us back to the present, but with meditation and other exercises, mindful awareness of the present can also be learned. It's taken me all these years to put this together, but I'm now convinced that the real reason radio studios have always been such safe havens for me is that because, in them, I have no choice but to focus on the moment. There's simply no option other than to give my full attention to what I'm doing live on the air.

There is one final aspect of my *releasing* and *finding faith* practices that I want to mention here, and it's one that you might not tend to associate with either: medication. As you've now read, I long fought the idea of taking an SSRI or any other pill known to help obsessive-compulsives. I couldn't see this back in the '90s, but I now know there were two successive reasons for this. Initially, like many OCs, I was worried about losing that much more control of my life (by being "drugged") and my identity (by losing my non-pill-popping status as a "normal" person). Then later, as I became determined to understand the mechanics of belief, I somehow concluded that taking medication was a spiritual cop-out, for lack of a better term.

I was wrong, very wrong, on both counts.

Medication is not a panacea in battling OCD, nor is it a substitute for the all the requisite work. It can, however, be an extremely effective tool for OCs to *gain*—not lose—control of their lives, by medically helping in the biophysical process of releasing stuck thoughts. Call it another OCD paradox.

As for the notion that taking pills somehow shows a lack of faith in a higher power, I'm now certain that notion is seriously flawed. At the risk of offending anyone with differing beliefs, I must say that *I've* come to believe that science and spirituality are much like our own two feet, each dependent on the other to move us forward. By accepting this idea and all that modern medicine has to offer, I now know I can do so much more to serve my own greater good.

Keep perspective, take initiative, and *release and have faith.* These are my coping strategies to this day, and I know that together they are the real gifts of my year-long project—an experiment in believing of which I will always treasure each and every minute, including the last. . .

▶ *11:59 p.m., October 21, 1998.*
PLAY　　It's so still in the room now that I can hear the hands on my wristwatch meet up at the

twelve. I can hear the click of my illusory tape re-corder running out of tape.

Never before has "This Is It" felt more true.

I write the three words on my index card, and just to make sure I get the very *last* word in on Doubt, I whisper two more:

I believe.

epilogue

fast-forward 7 years

March 21, 2006. It's a Tuesday morning and I am headed out the door of our new home in the North Bay hills, overlooking the outer reaches of the San Francisco Bay. The skies are overcast and about to open up, so I decide it's best not to drop the top of my Mazda Miata. No problem, though; I no longer *need* to.

Buying a used pint-sized convertible had been part of my strategy to get myself back behind the wheel of a car on a regular basis. Without a roof over my head, I'd reasoned, I could see and hear everything around me that much better. I was right, and for well over a year, in all weather conditions, I drove almost everywhere with the top down, eliciting some rather interesting looks and comments along the way.

"Dude, you must be freezing your *ass* off," shouted the guy in the big 4-by-4 next to me at a red light one frosty winter morning.

"No, really, it's not *that-t-t-t* bad," I yelled back through chattering teeth.

I can't help smiling as I think about all this now, driving—top *and* windows up—to the nearby ferry terminal, where I'll catch my boat to San Francisco.

I pull into the ferry parking lot with a mere five minutes to spare. I grab my backpack and allow myself one quick inventory. Parking brake. Locks. Lights. Windows. *One, two, three, four/I can leave/I know the score.* I walk away without a single glance back.

Fifty minutes, a cup of coffee, and a *San Francisco Chronicle* later, I arrive in the City and walk to a nearby Peet's for another cup of coffee. I hand the barista a five, realizing I never did wash my hands after that sneeze (into my sleeve) on the ferry ride over. I'm okay.

Crossing the busy Embarcadero next, I join the pack of office workers and tourists who step off the curb before the walking light officially turns green. I have broken the rules. And I'm okay.

Now I'm feeling cocky, so I make a point of stepping on every manhole cover and sewer grating I pass along the ten blocks to work, even pausing to say hello to a friend *under* the scaffolding just outside our building. My pulse is rising quickly at this point, but I'm okay.

Finally, I arrive at 865 Battery Street. San Francisco headquarters for the CBS Radio and Television Network. I take the elevator to the third-floor newsroom, where soon the easy part of my day will begin, as I join my partner in Studio A and spend five hours co-anchoring afternoon drive, as I've been doing every weekday now for a year and half.

Like most days, I'm tempted to pinch myself, or at least to take a minute to remember just how blessed I am: To be back at KCBS. To be back in cars. To be back inside crowded places. To be back at Christmas tree farms and around children again. To be back as a husband and father.

To be back.

■

March 21 is a good day. Not all my days are so chock full of OCD successes. Truth is, my battles with Doubt are never-ending. More often than not I am strong enough to defend myself. But not always. There are still those moments of weakness when I get stuck at a sink, or loop my car in a circle, or check and re-check a door or a parking brake, or play back a portion of the airchecks I have yet to stop myself from recording.

The difference now is that I know my way *out* of Doubt's grip. I know how to believe beyond the flawed processing of my own physical senses. And I also know how to accept the many gifts of support available to me. I have learned to put stubborn pride aside and ask for help, from Jackie and others, when I need it. And, as I've attempted to explain, I have made peace with medication, coming to understand how it helps me function, and thereby helps me serve my greater good.

■

I am awed by, and forever grateful for, the way in which my project has influenced not only me, but also so many others in my life. Nicole and Brianna, now fifteen and twelve, have grown up with their own handmade belief models on their nightstands, and for years Samantha and I have used the twelve "pyramid words" to give our family a common vocabulary for talking about the power of believing—in ourselves, in others, and in life. The dozen words also adorn a bathroom mirror at my sister's home, and her daughters too have grown up talking about such principles as *Passion* and *Integrity* and *Faith* and *Release*.

For nine years now, Carole Johnson and I have met often for coffee, to share our OCD triumphs and challenge one another to take that next step. For Carole, it's been travel, which she'd given up at the demand of her own Doubt monster. And for me, it's been finding the courage to move this book forward. Today, Carole is taking cruises, and I am gearing up for book tours ahead. We both tend to shake our heads in disbelief that much more with every get-together, one of the most recent of which included a quick ride in the Miata. "You drove me, Jeff!" Carole marveled as we pulled back into my driveway—just before she got out of the car and closed the door very deliberately, with a huge smile on her face. It took me a minute to figure out what she'd just done: shut the door not three times, but only once!

And then there's the magic of what this book project has done to bring the family I grew up with together again. For the first time ever, we're talking about the elephant in the room, the scarring perfectionism that so often drove us apart. We are all committed, as parents and grandparents, to seeing that none of our next generation ever feels pressured to do anything "just right." The brutal honesty of all this is uncomfortable at times, but no one has encouraged me more than my father to tell my story just as I remember it: to hold nothing back that might be helpful to others. That, and our renewed friendship, are two of the greatest gifts I could ask for.

■

We in the news business sometimes opt to "sit on" a story, which is to say we occasionally choose *not* to report on something if there's a compelling reason to keep it under wraps.

As my voice of doubt points out to me daily, there are at least a thousand reasons—all of them compelling—why I should sit on my story.

But I can't. I owe far too much to far too many.

My OCD story is hardly a typical one, if there is such a thing. I have battled a more severe form of doubt than most obsessive-compulsives I've read about. And I have taken an especially circuitous path to recovery, drawing on resources both inside and outside the traditional mental health field. What worked for me might very well prove entirely ineffective for another OC. Still, I know firsthand the power of shared stories, and I wonder to this day where I'd be if not for the personal accounts I read in *The Boy Who Couldn't Stop Washing*, and the tales I heard from a handful of recovering drunks and addicts determined to make something of their lost years. It's in this spirit that I am committed to sharing my own story, hoping it might, in whatever small way, help not only other OCs, but anyone who's ever struggled with doubt.

And besides, a bargain's a bargain.

Author's Note

There may be no greater measure of my OCD recovery than the length of these final comments I'm compelled to share.

Eight years ago when I first set out to turn my stacks of index cards into a book, I battled my way past Doubt by promising myself I'd write a thirty-page disclaimer qualifying each and every thing I had to say, imploring readers to avoid drawing any meaningful conclusions from my experiences.

Doubt would still like me to do this. And more.

Were I fully recovered, I suppose I might flat-out refuse.

I can't.

But I can, and I will, force myself to say everything I still need to say within the confines of the next three paragraphs:

Rewind, Replay, Repeat is a work of nonfiction: an account of actual events in my life. It is also, however, a memoir, meaning its pages are filled, first and foremost, with my memories—recollections that might best be hedged by disclaimers such as "As best I can recall . . ." or "While I can't remember the particulars. . ." My early drafts were filled with such qualifiers. Over the years, though, I have forced myself to remove all this clutter and allow my imagination to fill in the holes in my memory while re-creating scenes and conversations as best I can. Moreover, I have knowingly altered names and personal characteristics, and have made occasional minor changes to details and chronology for the sake of clarity. To avoid confusion, I have also made consistent use of two labels which, in reality, evolved over many years: *Doubt* (with a capital "D"), to refer to the source of my obsessive *what-if?* questions; and *tapes* to refer to all my mental reviews.

These liberties, though entirely insignificant to the heart of my story, are nonetheless pure blasphemy to a precision-obsessed OCD checker like myself. What fascinates and encourages me, though, is this: while I may yet obsess over my story in years to come, at this moment, I am more certain about the contents of this clearly imperfect "recording" than I am about the material on any of the countless cassette airchecks I've played back over and over again in the past.

I think it has something to do with learning how to believe in one's heart, even while doubting one's head.

Afterword

Some Final Thoughts from Jeff's Therapist

By Jacqueline B. Persons, Ph.D.

It is rare to be privy to the details of a patient's experience of his therapy, and to follow it over time as Jeff permits me—and his readers—to do in this very moving book. I generally get a grainy snapshot of my patients' experiences in therapy, a snapshot limited both in time and vantage point. Just *how* limited I learned by reading this book! I was surprised to discover in these pages how much difficulty Jeff had doing his exposure homework—that is, exercises to expose himself to the situations he feared. This information helped me understand why Jeff suffered for so long. Cognitive behavioral therapy (CBT) is typically quite effective, and I frequently felt surprised by Jeff's prolonged suffering. Now I understand why he didn't benefit from the therapy for a long time. He wasn't really doing it! As he notes, when Jeff began working aggressively to confront his fears, he began to recover.

Jeff is a persistent and hard-working person, as this book makes quite clear. His difficulty carrying out his treatment says a lot about the therapies we have to offer our patients with OCD. They are extremely—even excessively—demanding. Exposure-based treatment requires the patient to confront exactly the things he fears most! The field must develop therapies that are easier for patients to carry out. We are now beginning to do that. Jeff describes some of the cognitive and mindfulness interventions, developed by Jeffrey Schwartz and others, that are much easier to use and are beginning to be supported by evidence of effectiveness.

Reading this book was a humbling experience. Certainly it shows CBT's key role in Jeff's recovery. But it also shows that CBT was only one of many pieces of a large puzzle. Other pieces included other therapies (including medication) and therapists, and support of many kinds from many places, including from Jeff's family and from others in his community.

Jeff relied on his initiative, intelligence, persistence, stamina, and his considerable problem-solving and interpersonal skills. He has a strong spiritual life. All played a role in his recovery. Timing was also important; it often happens that a strategy that was not helpful at one time might be invaluable at another.

The spiritual approach to OCD that Jeff developed deserves special mention. As he indicates, I was initially quite skeptical. Raised as a pragmatic Midwesterner, I am probably the least spiritual person in the universe. And spiritual work was not an evidence-based intervention for OCD! I feared that Jeff's spiritual strategies were OCD rituals in sheep's clothing. I learned from Jeff how therapeutic spiritual concepts and methods could be. In fact, these ideas are now entering the scientific mainstream, as described in books by Steve Hayes and Dan Wegner. A linchpin of Jeff's spiritual approach was the appeal to a higher good as a rationale for letting go of fears and urges to ritualize. Instead of trying to eliminate obsessions, Jeff focused on his values and life goals. In Hayes's words, Jeff asked: "Can I feel and think what I feel and think and still act?" Jeff could and did, as he demonstrates in many ways, including by courageously writing this remarkable book.

■

Jacqueline B. Persons, Ph.D., is director of the San Francisco Bay Area Center for Cognitive Therapy. She is also an associate clinical professor in the Department of Psychology at the University of California, Berkeley.

Suggested Reading by Authors Noted Above

Hayes, S. C., and S. Smith. *Get Out of Your Mind and Into Your Life: The New Acceptance and Commitment Therapy.* Oakland, CA: New Harbinger, 2005.

Schwartz, J. M. *Brain Lock: Free Yourself from Obsessive-Compulsive Behavior.* New York: ReganBooks/HarperCollins, 1996.

Wegner, D. M. *White Bears and Other Unwanted Thoughts: Suppression, Obsession, and the Psychology of Mental Control.* New York: Guilford, 1994.

Acknowledgments

Just how does one go about thanking the people who've helped him not only write a book, but also rescue a life? I can't imagine. What I *do* know is that I owe my eternal gratitude to the following people who've done so much in both regards.

My angel: Carole Johnson. The Talmud tells us that every blade of grass has an angel leaning over it, whispering, "Grow, grow." For nearly a decade now, Carole, you have provided that steady whisper in my life. Without you, this book would not exist. Because of you, I know all things are possible.

My rocks: Mandi and Mike Friedel. Mandi, draft

after draft, revision after revision, you have been there with me, guiding, encouraging, and gently challenging me. Make the book a metaphor for my recovery, and the same statement holds equally true. Your generosity inspires and humbles me. Mike, thank you for your love and friendship, and for all you've unwittingly taught me about "quiet confidence."

My roots: Mom and Dad. You two will never know how much I appreciate your unconditional support of this project. By encouraging me to share my story just as I remember it, and *without* holding anything back, you paved the way for me to reach deep into my soul. I can't think of a greater gift any parents could offer.

My mentors: John Christgau, Wayne Manning, and Michael Moran. Thank you for showing me, each through your own life and work, just who and what it is I aspire to be.

My book team. Thank you, Susan Schulman, for lending me your vision and wisdom; Becky Post, for opening Hazelden Publishing's doors to me and making me feel so welcome inside; Mindy Keskinen, for giving this project your expert care; Dr. Jackie Persons, for committing yourself to my recovery *and* this book; Drs. Jeffrey Schwartz, Judith Rapoport, and Jerry Jampolsky, for inspiring and supporting me; Joanna Mendoza, for always being there; and Richard Marek, Wayne Davis, Valerie Upham,

Mindy Harding, and Patricia Perkins, for sharing your invaluable feedback.

My radio family. Thank you, Kitty O'Neal, Chris Lane, and Patti Reising, three of the finest on-air partners, and off-air friends, I could ever ask for; my immensely talented KCBS colleagues, with whom I'm privileged to work; and the legendary Charles Osgood, whose generous support for this book means the world to me.

My extended family. Thank you, Zaida, for nurturing me; Bethany, Katie, Joy, Dick, Melissa, Scott, Miranda, Rachel, Jan, Moco, and Ralph, for enriching my life in so many ways; Cathleen, for encouraging me, again and again; Bud, Frankie, and Chad, for sharing *your* angel with me; and everyone at Spiritual Life Center in Sacramento, for providing me the safest home in the world.

And most of all, my best friends: Samantha, Nicole, Brianna (and Zaxi). Thank you for believing in me, long before I, myself, could. You are my everything, and I'll love you forever.

OCD Resources

Obsessive Compulsive Foundation
676 State Street
New Haven, CT 06511
203-401-2070
www.ocfoundation.org

National Institute of Mental Health
NIMH Public Inquiries
6001 Executive Blvd., Room 8184, MSC 9663
Bethesda, MD 20892-9663
301-443-4513
www.nimh.nih.gov

References

Chapter 8

Foa, Edna B., and Reid Wilson. *Stop Obsessing! How to Overcome Your Obsessions and Compulsions*. New York: Bantam Books, 1991.

Neziroglu, F., and J. A. Yaryura-Tobias. *Over and Over Again: Understanding Obsessive-Compulsive Disorder*, revised edition. New York: Lexington Books, 1995.

Rapoport, Judith. *The Boy Who Couldn't Stop Washing*. New York: Penguin, 1991.

Steketee, Gail S., and Kerrin White. *When Once Is Not Enough: Help for Obsessive-Compulsives*.

Oakland, CA: New Harbinger Publications, 1990.

Chapter 10

Baer, Lee. *Getting Control: Overcoming Your Obsessions and Compulsions*. New York: Penguin/ Plume, 1992.

Chapter 12

Beck, A. T., A. J. Rush, B. F. Shaw, and G. Emery. *Cognitive Therapy of Depression*. New York: Guilford Press, 1979.

Chapter 13

Foundation for Inner Peace. *A Course in Miracles*. Glen Ellen, CA: 1975.

Jampolsky, Gerald G., and Diane Cirincione. *Change Your Mind, Change Your Life*. New York: Bantam Books, 1993.

Jampolsky, Gerald G. *Love Is Letting Go of Fear*. Berkeley, CA: Celestial Arts, 1979.

Chapter 16

Source for the Twelve Steps:

Alcoholics Anonymous. *Alcoholics Anonymous,* fourth edition. New York: Alcoholics Anonymous World Services, Inc., 2001.

Chapter 17
Schwartz, Jeffrey M. *Brain Lock: Free Yourself from Obsessive-Compulsive Behavior.* New York: ReganBooks/HarperCollins, 1996.

Chapter 18
Covey, Stephen R. *The Seven Habits of Highly Effective People.* New York: Simon & Schuster, 1990.

Chapter 26
Bunyan, John. *Grace Abounding to the Chief of Sinners.* Penguin Classics edition, W. R. Owens, editor. New York: Penguin, 1987.
Ciarrocchi, Joseph W. *The Doubting Disease: Help for Scrupulosity and Religious Compulsions.* Mahwah, NJ: Paulist Press, 1995.

Chapter 27
Fox, Emmet. *The Golden Key.* Special Unity Edition. Unity Village, MO: Unity Books, 1944.

Chapter 29
Schwartz, Jeffrey M. *Brain Lock.*
Dyer, Wayne W. *Your Sacred Self: Making the Decision to Be Free.* New York: HarperCollins, 1995.

About the Author

Jeff Bell is a longtime veteran of radio and television news. He currently co-anchors afternoons at KCBS Radio in San Francisco, one of the most successful all-news radio stations in America. His extensive media experience includes nearly a decade of anchoring drive-time radio programs, several years of writing television news, and numerous days spent chasing stories throughout Northern California. He lives in the Bay Area with his wife and two daughters. Jeff Bell is an air-name.

Visit Jeff online at:

www.RewindReplayRepeat.com

Hazelden Publishing is a division of the Hazelden Foundation, a not-for-profit organization. Since 1949, Hazelden has been a leader in promoting the dignity and treatment of people afflicted with the disease of chemical dependency.

The mission of the foundation is to improve the quality of life for individuals, families, and communities by providing a national continuum of information, education, and recovery services that are widely accessible; to advance the field through research and training; and to improve our quality and effectiveness through continuous improvement and innovation.

Stemming from that, the mission of this division is to provide quality information and support to people wherever they may be in their personal journey—from education and early intervention, through treatment and recovery, to personal and spiritual growth.

Although our treatment programs do not necessarily use everything Hazelden publishes, our bibliotherapeutic materials support our mission and the Twelve Step philosophy upon which it is based. We encourage your comments and feedback.

The headquarters of the Hazelden Foundation are in Center City, Minnesota. Additional treatment facilities are located in Chicago, Illinois; Newberg, Oregon; New York, New York; Plymouth, Minnesota; and St. Paul, Minnesota. At these sites, we provide a continuum of care for men and women of all ages. Our Plymouth facility is designed specifically for youth and families.

For more information on Hazelden, please call 1-800-257-7800 or visit us at www.hazelden.org.

Other titles that may interest you:

Get Me Out of Here
My Recovery from Borderline Personality Disorder
Rachel Reiland

A mother, wife, and working professional, Reiland was diagnosed with BPD at age twenty-nine—which finally explained her explosive anger, manipulative behaviors, and self-destructive episodes. In this memoir she reveals what the disorder looks and feels like, and how she healed through intensive therapy and support.
Softcover, 464 pp.
Order No. 2138

Today I Will Do One Thing
Daily Readings for Awareness and Hope
Especially for those diagnosed with dual disorders, this resource offers daily insight and strength.
Softcover, 416 pp.
Order No. 1400

Hazelden

Hazelden books are available at fine bookstores everywhere. To order directly from Hazelden, call 1-800-328-9000 or visit www.hazelden.org/bookstore.